PATIO &
WALKWAY
IDEAS THAT WORK

LEE ANNE WHITE

The Taunton Press

The Taunton Press
Inspiration for hands-on living®

The Taunton Press, Inc.,
63 South Main Street, PO Box 5506
Newtown, CT 06470-5506
e-mail: tp@taunton.com

Editor: Carolyn Mandarano
Copy editor: Marc Sichel
Indexer: Jim Curtis
Interior design: Carol Petro
Layout: Susan Lampe-Wilson
Illustrator: Christine Erikson
Cover Photographers: (Front cover, clockwise from top left): © Jennifer Cheung Photography; © Chris Giles; © Brian Vanden Brink;
© Jennifer Cheung Photography; © Eric Roth; (Back cover, clockwise from top left): © Brian Vanden Brink; © Eric Roth; © Mark Lohman;
© Lee Ann White; © Jennifer Cheung Photography; © Mark Lohman

Library of Congress Cataloging-in-Publication Data
White, Lee Anne.
  Patio & walkway ideas that work / Lee Anne White.
     p. cm.
  Includes index.
  ISBN 978-1-60085-483-5
1. Patios—Design and construction. 2. Courtyards—Design and construction. I. Title. II. Title: Patio and walkway ideas that work.
  TH4970.W463 2012
  690'.184—dc23
                              2012028688

Printed in the United States of America
10 9 8 7 6 5

ACKNOWLEDGMENTS

What makes a great idea book is not so much the writing as the ideas presented. And for that, I thank the many designers located across the country whose work is showcased throughout this book. Among them are a handful of designers that deserve special recognition for their assistance with this project. Their insight, creativity, and projects have helped bring this book to life: Catherine Clemens of Clemens & Associates, Inc.; Mark Fockele and Stephanie Gordon of The Fockele Garden Company; Cassy Aoygi of FormLA; Katie Fragan of Katie Moss Landscape Design; Lisa North and Andre Del Re of Da Vida Pools; and landscape architects Richard McPherson and Jeni Webber.

Of course, we couldn't feature these projects without photographs. In addition to my own images, the book features the work of eight very talented photographers: Brian Vanden Brink, Chris Giles, Eric Roth, Mark Lohman, Jennifer Cheung, Mick Hales, Steven Nilsson, and Susan Teare. Thanks, also, to the many homeowners who allowed their patios and walkways to be photographed.

To the great staff at Taunton Books, I extend my heartfelt appreciation for more than 12 years of collaboration on book projects. I am especially thankful for my editor, Carolyn Mandarano, who I have known since my magazine days at The Taunton Press and with whom I have worked closely on many projects over the years. It continues to be a pleasure. Thanks also to Taunton's photo editor, Katy Binder, for her good nature, resources, and support.

And finally, for simply "being there" and for their assistance while working on this project and photographing landscapes for inclusion, I would like to thank Alan White, Tawny Kern, Alison Sellers, and Whitney Cochran. They never fail to brighten each day.

CONTENTS

INTRODUCTION

I've spent the past 15 years traversing our country—photographing residential gardens and landscape architecture and visiting with homeowners and designers alike. In doing so, I'm constantly inspired by the creativity and ingenuity that go into the design and construction of outdoor spaces. This is especially true when it comes to patios and outdoor rooms. Let's just say that these aren't the patios I grew up with (although I have fond memories of time spent in those much simpler spaces, too).

Sometimes, instead of heading back to my hotel room after a photo shoot, I have been invited to stay for dinner or drinks. It has been during these times that I get to see how these outdoor spaces are really used and just how much they are enjoyed. Sometimes, it is clear that great thought has been placed into planning the dinner. Other times, the meals are thrown together at the last minute, and I've had the pleasure of helping out by setting the table, keeping an eye on the grill, or pouring the wine. I have cherished these evenings—for the delicious food, which is often fresh from the garden, for the camaraderie and conversation, and for the chance to relax among new friends. These dinners have outshined even the best of restaurants I've had the chance to experience along the way.

The truth is, there is just something magical about cooking, dining, and entertaining outdoors. The food tastes better. The atmosphere is more relaxed. Whether watching the sun set or the stars twinkle, a patio is a great place to unwind. It's also a great place to start the day with your morning coffee or to take a break at midday, perhaps while your children play in the yard. A comfortable patio is simply a great place to be—whether you're spending a few quiet moments alone or visiting with your daughter, an old friend, or a new acquaintance.

Although often overlooked, just as important as the outdoor spaces we enjoy are the pathways that lead to them, as well as to the home and other spaces in the landscape. They are part of the journey and help set the tone for a great experience. Because they are often built at the same time, with many of the same materials and using most of the same basic construction techniques, it makes sense to include them when talking about patios.

In this book, we'll take a look at what makes patios and pathways comfortable, functional, safe, and inviting. We'll explore some of the keys to designing great outdoor spaces and showcase innovative ideas for outdoor rooms, outdoor kitchens, poolside patios, and more. And you'll learn about working collaboratively with design professionals to create the kinds of spaces that suit your unique needs, interests, lifestyle, and budget. The goal is to help you make the best choices for your outdoor space.

DESIGN FOR

A well-designed patio is an invitation to enjoy

the great outdoors in your own backyard.

THE WAY

It's a place to unwind, entertain,

or spend time with family.

YOU LIVE

Lifestyles vary from one place and person to another. Some regions of the country are geared toward al fresco living almost year-round, while the season for spending time outdoors may be quite short in others. Some homeowners enjoy entertaining outdoors, while others prefer a quiet space in which to unwind. Families may need a range of outdoor spaces for growing children and a place where parents can comfortably keep an eye on them. Whatever your lifestyle, a patio serves as a focal point for outdoor living and can be easily adapted to your needs.

The best place to begin the planning process is by exploring the ways in which you might use your outdoor space. Obvious options include cooking, dining, relaxing, entertaining, and gardening. But be specific, and include each member of the family in the planning process. Here are some questions to get you thinking:

- Will you most often cook for a couple, a family, or two dozen friends?

- Do you want some low-maintenance landscape plants to green up your outdoor space or do you wish to indulge a passion for container gardening?

- Would you use an outdoor fireplace to extend your season—knocking off the chill on evenings—or would you simply retreat indoors?

- What would make a patio more inviting to you—a soothing water feature, colorful plantings, open views, or tall privacy walls?

- Would you rather gather around a table with friends, curl up in a cushy chair with a good book, or snooze in a hammock?

Beyond thinking about your family's needs and wants, consider your guests, too, especially if you entertain a lot. Will you want bar seating where friends can keep you company while you cook? What about a table where kids or adults can play games? A sandbox for young children tucked into one corner? Start by dreaming of your ideal outdoor environment. Having a general concept and list of ideas provides a perfect starting point when meeting with a designer.

Start with an Idea File

When it comes to adding a patio to your home, part of the fun is the time you spend thinking about and visualizing your space. So before you meet with a designer, take some time to daydream, gather ideas, and make notes. Create an idea box or idea file, and fill it with photos, clippings, sketches, notes, color samples, or anything that you find inspirational. Good sources for ideas include magazines, books, and catalogs of all kinds. But don't stop there. Go on garden tours and take snapshots of spaces, amenities, and construction details that you like. Download images and information from the Web. Pick up paint samples at the local home center. Visit a stone center or brickyard to purchase or photograph samples of construction materials you like. That way, when you sit down with your designer, you'll have a valuable visual reference for sharing your vision and ideas.

top • Designed for cooking and dining al fresco, this courtyard patio features a full-service outdoor kitchen with a full-sized sink, bar tap, under-counter refrigerator, grill, and side burner. Wall-mounted lights illuminate the cooking area, and a table offers guests a place to visit and dine.

above • A mix of covered and uncovered spaces enable these homeowners to combine their passions for art and outdoor living. The outdoor kitchen is tucked beneath the eave, while patio space spills out onto the terrace below.

left • The deep-seated Adirondack chairs issue an invitation to relax and linger on this cut-bluestone patio. From here, parents can keep an eye on lakeside activities, soak up the sun, and enjoy the sunset.

Connecting Spaces and Creating Transitions

In addition to planning your outdoor spaces, also think about how you move into, through, and out of these spaces. Sometimes spaces are adjacent—such as a patio that flows from a living room without a grade change. Other times, spaces must be connected by pathways—whether it's from the driveway to the front door, the front yard to the backyard, or the patio to the pool. How these paths are designed says a lot about their purpose.

Formal paths—those that are wider, often mortared, and feature higher-quality materials—are most at home out front. Sturdily built utilitarian paths are the workhorses of the landscape, connecting the house to various destinations and these destinations to each other. And then there are the casual garden paths—those narrow, winding paths made of loose materials or steppingstones, often just wide enough for one person—that provide access to the garden or more remote spaces in the landscape.

top • Although both patios are paved in brick, they are clearly distinguished as different spaces—one for dining, the other for gardening—by the narrow, connecting steppingstone path and the vine-covered arch set atop brick posts.

bottom • Cut-stone pavers have been widely spaced in the grass alongside a broad patio to provide access to other points in the landscape. The contrast in paving styles adds a strong graphic element to the formal landscape.

When you step from one space into another—say, from the house to the patio or from the patio to a path—you move through a transitional space. Transitional spaces deserve special attention as they help set the mood and tone in the landscape. They may be signaled by a grade change, an upright structure such as an arbor or gate, the narrowing or widening of a path, or a simple change in the materials underfoot—such as stepping from a paved surface onto the lawn or from brick to stone. Or they may be simply framed by trees and other plantings. Spaces that connect without a grade change offer a sense of safety, flow, and accessibility. Grade changes can add considerable interest to outdoor spaces.

Aesthetic, functional, and safety considerations all play into the design of transitional spaces—especially when they involve grade changes. Wide, straight passageways provide easier access and a strong sense of formality. Narrow, winding passageways are more casual and create a sense of intrigue.

top · This irregularly laid, meandering staircase is far more interesting than most straight staircases. It calls attention to the surrounding garden and the experience of passage while serving a utilitarian purpose.

bottom · This passageway serves as a kind of "entrance hall" connecting the driveway to the backyard patio. It is designed to be passed through, but the water feature, wall, and sculpture make it an interesting place to pause, as well.

Working with Designers

No matter what space you're designing, when it comes to design, collaboration is key. Smart designers take the time to understand and address a homeowner's needs, lifestyle, vision, and budget. It is equally important for homeowners to be smart about choosing and working with a designer. This will help ensure a professional working relationship and enable you, the homeowner, to take advantage of the designer's ideas, experience, and expertise.

The first step is choosing the right professional. The size, complexity, and budget of a project all play into making that choice. There is significant overlap in the areas of expertise among professionals, but on a sliding scale, garden designers are generally suited to smaller projects with a strong emphasis on plantings while residential landscape architects are trained and licensed to handle larger, more complex outdoor design and construction projects. Landscape designers often fall somewhere in between, providing a wide range of design and installation services, while landscape contractors tend to focus on activities such as grading, construction, and the installation of drainage, irrigation, landscape lighting, and plants.

But even within these categories, services vary and designers have their own areas of specialty. Ask to see samples of their work that may be similar in scope and style to your project and contact several references. Find out how the professionals work, how long they expect it will take to complete your project, and how they charge for their services.

Once you've chosen a design professional, share your wish list and vision. Be open and honest about your budgets and expectations. And then be open to the ideas they present as well. Designers bring a fresh perspective and a wealth of creative problem-solving experience to every job. Let them introduce you to new materials and design ideas that you might never have imagined.

right • **This quiet retreat for one is the perfect place to land with a favorite book on a warm spring afternoon. The homeowners worked with an architect to create the larger, more formal entertaining pavilion.**

left • **The three sides of this house create a cozy atmosphere on this patio. Separate doors provide access to the living room (center), kitchen (left), and bedroom wing (right) for easy access from any part of the house.**

Sustainability Considerations

Sustainable landscapes are those that support environmental quality and help conserve our natural resources. By applying a few basic design principles, sustainable landscapes can be equally as beautiful, more cost effective, and easier to maintain than traditional landscapes. In fact, one of the guiding principles of sustainable landscaping is that, once established, the landscape should largely take care of itself.

Start by selecting materials wisely and using only what you need. Pave only as much ground as truly required to meet your needs; use local materials that look at home in the landscape and don't have to be shipped long distances; select from sustainably produced or harvested materials; and consider durable recycled materials. Broken concrete and recycled bricks, for instance, can be used effectively to create attractive and durable walls.

Pay special attention to water conservation. Consider paving options that allow rainwater to easily soak back into the soil, such as dry-laid rather than mortared construction techniques and materials such as gravel or permeable concrete pavers. Choose primarily native, adapted, or drought-tolerant plants that do not need to be watered once established. If supplemental irrigation is still necessary, group plants according to their watering needs, choose drip irrigation over sprinkler systems whenever possible, and turn off irrigation timers when there is adequate rainfall.

Minimize the use of lawns—using them only where needed most, such as play spaces for children—choosing alternative low-maintenance ground covers instead. This will greatly reduce the need for mowing, blowing, watering, and applying chemical fertilizers, herbicides, and pesticides. Also, reuse materials on site. Recycle excavated soil to fill holes or create planted berms that serve as wind buffers and screening. Choose plants that don't need to be pruned, and turn clippings into compost that can be used on site.

above • Rather than the usual permeable materials such as sand, granite fines, mulch, or even grass, the joints between the large, rectangular pavers on this patio are filled with drought-tolerant, low-growing succulents for a dramatic effect.

left · This patio consists of only as many stones as truly needed and positions them in an interesting way. The patio is eye catching because it creates unusual negative space amid a swath of grass.

above · Granite fines and small, crushed gravel are combined to create a compact and permeable pathway. Flagstone steps mark grade changes every 5 to 7 ft., while small boulders help create a retaining wall and garden bed filled with flowering plants.

left · This retaining wall was built from recycled concrete paving, which often can be rescued from nearby construction projects. Light fixtures, such as the one hanging from the tree, can be found at antique and architectural-salvage stores.

A Sustainably Designed Courtyard

Tim Corfman and Mary Sorenson spent little time outdoors before working with landscape designer Jeni Webber to transform a struggling, thirsty lawn and dismal row of shrubs into an inviting Mediterranean-style courtyard garden reminiscent of those they had seen in southern Spain. Now they relax and entertain outdoors, and even grow some of their own food.

The task was to create a pleasing view from the kitchen window, screen a neighboring house from view, and create an outdoor sitting area. The courtyard does all of that and more, and it does so in a sustainable, earth-friendly way. The courtyard is anchored by a poured-concrete wall with a raised bed and fountain. By using high fly-ash concrete with an integral stain, the need to finish the wall with stucco was eliminated. Fly ash, a by-product of the coal industry, can replace up to 50 percent of the cement in concrete, significantly reducing greenhouse gas emissions. The raised bed is planted with a drought-tolerant, non-fruit-bearing olive tree, and a tall hedge was planted behind the wall for additional screening.

Rather than paving the courtyard, it was covered with 1½ in. of local decomposed granite, which is permeable in nature, allowing rainwater to soak back into the ground. The lawn was eliminated and, instead, the homeowners grow fruits, vegetables, and herbs in a boulder-edged raised bed and dozens of containers. They also shifted from spray irrigation to much more efficient drip irrigation. And by utilizing only a minimum of outdoor lighting and no uplighting, they minimize light pollution as well. It's a healthy, sustainable, and inviting environment in which to relax with family and friends.

above • The courtyard is filled with edibles. Vegetables, herbs, and fruits fill both the raised garden bed and the containers placed closer to the house. Tomatoes are the homeowners' favorite vegetable to grow and eat.

above • The poured-concrete courtyard wall supports a raised bed and water feature. Birds and frogs are attracted to the water, and the bubbling of the fountains helps create a serene environment. The wall color comes from an integral stain rather than stucco, and the lower walls double as seating.

Rather than using stone, brick, or other paving materials, the owners opted to cover their patio in granite fines— an affordable, locally available, low-maintenance, and attractive material that allows rainwater to soak back into the ground.

Budgeting Realistically

With so many options for materials and amenities, the cost of building a patio, terrace, courtyard, or front walkway varies significantly. In many cases, it can be comparable to adding on a room or series of rooms to a house—especially if you opt to include features such as outdoor hearths, kitchens, swimming pools, spas, or pergolas. (And that's without considering any new planting plans.) But it is also quite possible to build a small, yet inviting patio on a shoestring budget.

As with any building project, it is important to establish a realistic budget upfront and to review it carefully with any designers and contractors hired to help with the job. If they know the expectations, they can point you in the direction of appropriate materials. Many new products have been introduced in recent years running the gamut in terms of durability, elegance, and price. Of course, the best thing about these new options is that there are many quality products available at reasonable prices. Even if cut and mortared bluestone isn't in the budget, dry-laid flagstone can be a beautiful and natural alternative. A patterned surface could also be achieved with concrete or brick pavers. Similarly, there are cost savings to be found by using prefabricated or ready-made grilling islands, hearths, and spas instead of custom-built masonry units. Outdoor furniture also comes in a range of materials from resin and aluminum to powder-coated iron and teak.

One strategy that works for many is to implement a plan over several years—focusing first on paving, basic landscaping, and functional furniture. It can be disruptive to rip out and replace paving, as well as to install lines for water, gas, and electricity, so get any heavy construction work out of the way initially. As long as utility access has been planned out in advance, amenities such as grilling islands, outdoor hearths, and landscape lighting can be added later. Furniture can also be upgraded when budgets allow, and garden beds can be planted over time. Your designer can help you explore ways to make the most of your landscaping budget.

above · Solid materials, used simply, can create an elegant, long-lasting outdoor environment. This bluestone patio and wooden arbor exude a sense of classic style in keeping with the home's architecture.

right · By using local stone, the designer both created a patio that looks like it belongs in this landscape and kept material costs within reason. Patios should only be as large as needed to make the best use of materials.

DESIGNING

When it comes to design, think of a patio as an outdoor room

complete with floors, walls, ceilings, windows, and doors.

PATIOS AND

Then give it character with well-chosen

materials and furnishings.

TERRACES

Types of Patios

Patios fall into five general categories based on their location and construction. **Attached patios** are the most common—paved spaces that extend from the rooms of a home into the landscape. They may be built on grade, raised above grade, or as a series of terraces with retaining walls and steps on different grades. They may be broad and expansive or little more than a stoop with room for a side chair or two. **Freestanding patios** are those that are independent of a house, located elsewhere in the landscape. They are special destinations. They may be built on a single level or be terraced, and may include architectural features such as seat walls, retaining walls, or pergolas.

Courtyards, similar to attached patios, extend from or are surrounded by a house. They differ in that they are private spaces enclosed by walls—either freestanding walls, the walls of the house or, in most cases, some combination of the two. **Integrated patios** are part of the home's structure. They sit atop, extend out from, or are recessed into a house. Although they are an architectural element rather than landscape feature, they are designed based on the same principles and with the same materials. Rooftop and balcony patios, as well as verandahs, loggias, and porticos all fall into this category.

Poolside patios—often referred to as pool decks, even when they use paving rather than decking materials—may adjoin a house or be freestanding in the landscape. They may be built at ground level, raised above ground level, or designed as a series of terraces. They are unique in that they surround a swimming pool and are typically integrated into the construction of the pool itself.

Although it extends from the walls of the house, this portico is still located beneath its roofline. It is a favorite place to enjoy the sound of a gentle rain or to duck out of the sun on a hot summer afternoon. The overhang also helps shade adjoining rooms.

above • This infinity edge pool doubles as a reflecting pool, helping to create a serene atmosphere in a woodland garden setting. The soft-toned, irregularly shaped flagstone helps the patio blend in almost naturally with the surrounding landscape.

left • This dry-laid flagstone patio is located below and just a stone's throw from the deck. While it isn't far from the house, its small size and native woodland plantings help to create a cozy destination that almost feels like a mountain getaway—despite its in-town location.

Types of Patios

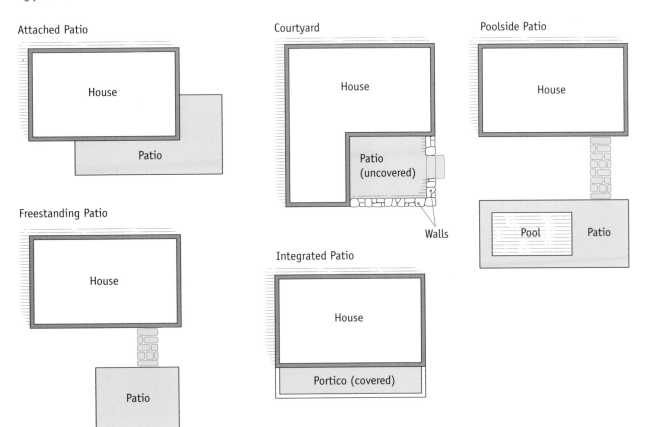

Attached Patio

House

Patio

Freestanding Patio

House

Patio

Courtyard

House

Patio (uncovered)

Walls

Integrated Patio

House

Portico (covered)

Poolside Patio

House

Pool Patio

Choosing the Right Location

While most patios are located just outside the back door, they can be equally at home throughout the landscape. A smart strategy is to build patios near rooms that serve similar functions. A patio for cooking and dining near the kitchen provides easy access to dishes, the refrigerator, a dishwasher, and sink. Broader spaces for gathering, as well as outdoor living rooms with patio furniture, can flow seamlessly from a living or family room, making a strong indoor-outdoor connection. Cozy patios for two are a delightful addition to any home when placed just beyond a master or guest bedroom. Front-yard patios are a lot like front porches in that they are welcoming in nature and help create a sense of community. Patios can be built around a pool for summertime fun or at a more distant location in the landscape to create an intriguing getaway. In an urban setting, a rooftop terrace may be a cherished destination.

A flat space is generally less expensive to build on than a hillside, which requires grading and the construction of retaining walls. Yet terraced patios are among the best ways to utilize a steep slope. Building patios adjacent to the house makes it easier to tap into plumbing, electricity, and gas lines for grills, outdoor kitchens, water features, and lighting. And before you get too far into the design process, be sure to check any local building codes and setback requirements that might impact your plans.

Also consider the relationship of your patio to the surrounding landscape. Are there special views that you'd like to preserve? Would placing a patio in a different location or shifting it slightly give you greater privacy from neighbors? What about sun, shade, and wind patterns during the time of year you will spend the most time outdoors? All of these considerations factor into your choice for a patio location.

above · Steep sites pose both challenges and opportunities. This one required considerable grading and the construction of an engineered stone retaining wall. Yet the lower patio works in perfect unison with an upper deck, providing an open and spacious area for dining, entertaining, and other outdoor activities.

left · This Cape Cod home is surrounded by a series of patios—some adjacent to the house, such as the stone patio with the seat wall in the foreground, and others located at a farther distance, such as the casual dining patio at the far edge of the lawn.

Evaluating Your Site

An easy and practical exercise that can help you evaluate potential sites for a patio calls for a chair, notepad, and pen. Place your chair in a location you are considering for your patio. Leave it there for a few days, returning at different times of day to sit, stand, walk around, and observe. Make notes on your pad, including the position of the chair. What do you see and hear? Does the space feel cozy, open, or overly exposed? Is it too hot, too cold, too windy, or just right? How would you describe your views? Do you want the views to be left open or framed, or does something need to be screened from view? How do you envision yourself spending time in this location? Is it a convenient location for the types of activities you would like to enjoy outdoors? After a few days, move your chair to a new location and complete the same evaluation process. After exploring multiple locations, chances are you'll have a strong sense for where to place your patio.

Before making a final decision, however, there are other practical matters to consider. These include the terrain or grade changes, as well as the shape and size of your property. Patios may also need to comply with building codes. In some municipalities, such codes limit the total area of land that can be occupied by structures or paved surfaces. Also, patios may be subject to setbacks, or the distance from your property line. It helps to have a site plan of your property showing the house, any existing structures, property lines, and setback distances. If your patio project incorporates a deck or swimming pool, building codes will almost certainly apply. A designer can help you identify and evaluate these details.

above · Although space was at a premium on this site, every square foot was maximized. The pool and pool deck are compact, but highly functional. The raised planting beds add dimension and double as seat walls. The focus is on quality rather than quantity, and attention has been given to details.

left · This rustic pergola is a compelling destination in the landscape. Not only does it exude charm, but it creates a sense of intrigue by implying—but not immediately revealing—a special view. Traversing the narrow path and steps to reach this destination helps build anticipation.

right · Don't overlook the front yard as a prime spot for a patio. The stone wall helps create a sense of enclosure for this small sitting area while remaining at a neighbor-friendly height. The space is brightened with colorful container plantings in pots and window boxes, as well as on stands.

Spaces that Relate to the House

When you walk through Jennifer and Bruce Miller's home, it's almost like walking along a garden path. They live in a mid-century modern, classic post-and-beam house with a Zen twist that features wall-to-wall windows along its length. These windows fill the house with light and look out onto a series of outdoor living and garden spaces.

The yard is narrow, unusually shaped, and surrounded by steep slopes. Neighbors' houses peer down from above. Yet the Millers love to entertain and wanted the space to feel open and welcoming. The challenge for the designers at FormLA™ was to create a sense of privacy without making the space feel closed in. The solution was to strategically plant tall bamboo where it would screen views, while creating a series of niches for different activities. These niches follow the outline of the house, closely connecting the indoors and out.

On one end are a covered dining area with a hearth and an outdoor kitchen with bar seating, which is located along a retaining wall. Both the bar and hearth are adorned with glass mosaic tile. Chocolate-colored flagstone paths lead to the central patio and garden, which features a bubbling fountain and chaise lounges. From there, the path leads to a bamboo alcove with gravel flooring and a day bed—a secret getaway where the homeowners retreat daily to bask in the sun, relax, and read.

Sound—which comes from the trickling of water, the crunch of gravel underfoot, and the swaying of the bamboo stalks—is an important aspect of this garden. It helps mask neighborhood noise, establish a serene setting, and create a sense of intrigue.

The backyard is a series of small, functional gathering spaces connected by flagstone paths. The fountain is a primary focal point that can be viewed from indoors as well as from several of the outdoor seating areas.

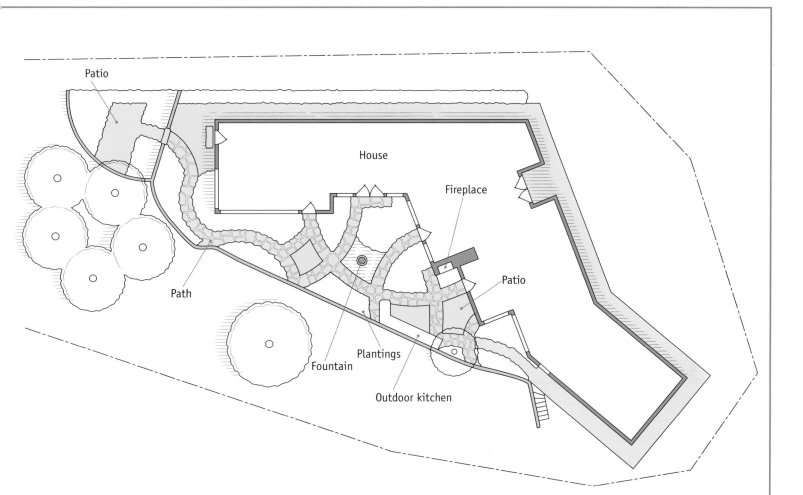

Patio

House

Fireplace

Patio

Path

Fountain

Plantings

Outdoor kitchen

left · This unique fire dish is recessed into a wall rather than placed out in the open. In addition to being highly decorative, the tiny glass tiles also reflect the heat back out into the covered patio, thus increasing the dish's efficiency.

left · The main dining space is located in the covered patio area with the fireplace, although additional bar seating is built against the retaining wall just past the outdoor kitchen. The bar also doubles as a buffet-style serving area and is a place to sit and work outdoors.

Creating a Comfortable Environment

When it comes to outdoor living spaces, comfort has to do with both your physical and psychological well-being. In other words, it relates to the overall sense of space as well as that space's functionality. And then there are the creature comforts—those simple luxuries like a good chair that have a lot to do with how long you may choose to stay in one place.

Start by considering your **climate.** While you may not have control over the weather, planning ahead for the most common local conditions can make your patio more inviting. If you live in a hot, humid part of the country, consider adding an overhead shade structure such as a portico, pergola, or awning—perhaps with a ceiling fan to create a cooling breeze and to help keep bugs at bay. If you crave the warmth of sunshine, select an open, sunny spot—perhaps around a swimming pool. If strong, prevailing winds are common, plant a tall evergreen hedge or build a courtyard wall to create a windbreak. And if you live in a rainy climate, consider constructing a solid roof overhead so that a sudden storm doesn't drive you indoors.

Think, too, about the **size** of the space. Are you more comfortable in a small, cozy space heavily screened for privacy or do you long for a broad, open view of the surrounding landscape? Perhaps a series of spaces—an outdoor kitchen, a dining room, and a gathering area near a cozy outdoor hearth—better suits your style.

Furnishings also have a lot to do with your comfort. Choose from a range of chairs, chaises, sofas, and benches made from a wide range of durable materials and covered with deep, soft cushions, if you like. Try them out for size, just as you would indoor furniture, to make sure they fit just right.

In hot, dry landscapes, offering respite from the brutal summer sun is essential. This outdoor dining area takes advantage of a shade tree, which acts as a ceiling above the table and chairs. It offers a comfortable alternative to the more protected gathering area located beneath the home's portal.

above • This outdoor gathering area is desirable for many reasons: The space is well-defined and modest in size yet very open to the lawn and garden. The teak chairs have soft cushions; some have footstools as well. And the fire adds a sense of both visual and physical warmth on cool evenings.

left • Filling this small space with fragrant herbs and flowering plants, a trickling wall fountain, and a generously cushioned chair creates a kind of secret garden for one, providing a peaceful refuge from work, shopping, and daily chores.

above · The colors are subtle, but the patterns and contrasting textures found in the patio paving, walls, fireplace, and containers help create an energizing space. It features numerous conversation pieces—from the tall papyrus-filled container to antiques to a "living" table covered in succulents.

far left · The stone fireplace is the primary focal point of this outdoor room, much as it would be in an indoor room. The biggest difference is that this is a multipurpose space—one used for cooking, dining, and gathering outdoors. The kitchen and hearth help form the walls and define its boundaries.

left · Covering walls and doorways with climbing vines transforms this outdoor room into a garden room. The vines soften the hard surfaces while providing an ever-changing, living element to the space. Planted containers and narrow planting beds help complete the setting.

10 Tips for Designing an Outdoor Room

1. **Make it convenient.** Out of sight is out of mind. If you can see it and easily access it from indoors, you're more likely to use it. Locate cooking and dining areas near the kitchen and areas for entertaining near family and living rooms. For destinations such as pools, make sure you have easily traversed pathways for getting there with supplies.

2. **Create a comfortable environment.** Patios and outdoor rooms are all about relaxing, so make yours casual and comfortable. Include the amenities you want and need most—whether a hammock, hearth, or fully equipped outdoor kitchen.

3. **Offer shelter from the elements.** In a hot climate, you'll appreciate the shade created by mature trees and shade structures such as pergolas, awnings, and umbrellas. Those with surfaces that shed rain can save a party from an unexpected shower. Walls, fences, and hedges can provide effective windbreaks.

4. **Screen for privacy and unwanted views.** If you'd rather not have neighbors or passersby eavesdropping on your conversations or checking out what's for dinner, screen your patio with hedges, trees, mixed plantings, walls, fences, or trellises. And don't forget overhead screening. A pergola or fabric canopies will block views from neighbors' decks and upstairs windows.

5. **Mask noises for a soothing setting.** Sometimes, it's nice to hear the sounds of a neighborhood. Other times, you really need something more soothing. A fountain will almost always do the trick.

6. **Use durable materials.** Low-maintenance, durable materials designed for outdoor use will make your life much easier. Choose materials that won't rust, rot, warp, peel, crack, or fade. Select furniture, lighting fixtures, ceiling fans, and outdoor kitchen cabinetry and appliances specifically built and rated for outdoor use.

7. **Install adequate lighting.** The most inviting outdoor spaces feature a mix of functional and accent lighting. Task lights brighten cooking and dining areas. Ambient lighting will create a warm and inviting atmosphere. Path and step lighting will allow you to move about safely. And spotlighting can highlight special elements such as water features, sculpture, or plantings that give a space character.

8. **Plan ahead for utilities.** Even if you don't use them initially, installing water, electricity, and gas lines before the paving is laid will save money and construction headaches later on. Keeping utility runs short will also cut costs, as will using portable propane tanks or charcoal grills on patios located farther from the house.

9. **Build everything to shed water.** Paths, patio flooring, overhead structures, and outdoor cabinetry should all be designed so that water will run off. Patios, pool decks, and other paved surfaces may need drainage systems as well. Weather-stripping and drains for outdoor kitchen cabinets are also a smart idea.

10. **Make it easy to winterize.** In cold climates, water and gas lines must be turned off when temperatures plummet. Making shut-off valves easily accessible will simplify winterization. Also, choose furnishings that are either designed for year-round outdoor use or are light enough to move to shelter for winter. Plan ahead for the convenient storage of cushions, furniture, and outdoor accessories.

Visualizing the Space

When we think of patios, paved surfaces are what often come to mind first. Yet a patio occupies three-dimensional space in the landscape and in relation to a house, not just a footprint on the ground. As such, it should be conceived with thoughts toward floors, walls, ceilings, passageways, and even "windows" into the landscape beyond. It may extend logically from a room of the home or wrap around a corner of a house to create a more interesting and integrated space. At its best, it is almost imperceptibly woven into the landscape—not just with gardens and lawns beyond, but within its boundaries, as well. Raised beds, planting pockets, vine-covered arbors, and container plantings can all be elements of patio design.

The materials used to construct a patio help set the tone and character of the space, whether formal, rustic, or contemporary in style. They add texture and color, warming up or adding a cooling element to any outdoor gathering area. Walls, fences, and plantings all help define the boundaries—whether tightly or loosely enclosed. A patio may be open to the sky, tucked beneath the eave of a portico, shaded by a mature tree, or sheltered by some other structure such as a pergola, awning, or colorful expanses of sailcloth.

Other elements—from furniture, sculpture, and containers to outdoor kitchens, hearths, and water features—also define the character of a patio, help break expanses of paving into more intimate spaces, and bring the patio to life. Outdoor lighting adds ambience in evenings while creating interesting shadows and highlights. So when you visualize a backyard patio, terraced hillside, entry courtyard, or rooftop patio, try thinking of it as an outdoor room with the potential for just as much character and personality as any room in your house. Also imagine yourself in this room—what you see, how you feel, and what you are doing. It's all part of the planning process.

This patio is a series of small spaces that seat two to four people—some covered and some open to the broad, southwest sky. A runnel, or water channel, divides two of the spaces. It connects to contemporary fountains on either end.

top right · This space was clearly visualized in three dimensions. What could have been a wooden deck is instead presented as a raised patio with an outdoor kitchen. The kitchen wall and raised-bed planters built of contrasting stone give a split-level look to the patio.

bottom right · Color, texture, and a casual, eclectic style combine to give this patio plenty of character. The finely textured gravel and plant foliage contrast with the smooth surfaces of the architectural fragments, bench, ceramic water jugs, and bistro table.

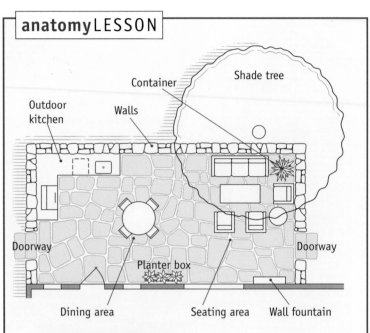

Container
Shade tree
Outdoor kitchen
Walls
Doorway
Doorway
Planter box
Dining area
Seating area
Wall fountain

OUTDOOR ROOM

Designing an outdoor room is, in many ways, similar to designing an indoor room. Although the scale and materials are different, most of the elements are the same.

FLOORS

- Decorative concrete
- Concrete pavers
- Stone, brick, tile
- Crushed stone, gravel

WALLS

- Privacy walls
- Seat walls
- Fences, lattice
- Shrubs, hedges, trees

CEILINGS

- Tree canopy
- Arbor, pergola, pavilion
- Umbrella, awning
- Porch or portico roof

PASSAGEWAYS

- Gates, posts
- Arbors, arches
- Paths, steps
- Plantings that frame entry

FURNISHINGS

- Tables, chairs, sofas
- Grilling islands, outdoor kitchens
- Fireplaces, fire pits
- Lighting
- Water features
- Sculpture, statuary, sundials
- Container plantings
- Electronics

left • The walls of this outdoor room—the house, the dark-green trellising, and the boxwoods—clearly define the boundaries of the space. The distinctive zigzagging herringbone pattern of the bricks resembles an area rug.

below • This outdoor room has the look and feel of an indoor room, only one wall is open to views and the weather. This impression was accomplished through the choice of furnishings, their arrangement, and accessories such as the lamps and ceiling fan.

Defining Boundaries

Whether open to the landscape beyond or enclosed on one or more sides, every patio has boundaries. Sometimes, the boundary is simply denoted by the edge of the paving—where it meets the lawn or other ground cover. Walls, fences, and plantings can serve as barriers, guardrails, and windbreaks; create a sense of intimacy and screen unwanted views; and add strong design elements such as dimension, color, and texture to an outdoor room. Even within the outer boundaries of a patio, additional internal boundaries can be established to break up the space into smaller, well-defined "rooms" with walls, planting beds, or rows of containers.

The character of a patio is often defined by the height and density of such boundaries. Walls, for instance, may be built at sitting height to create a sense of enclosure and definition while preserving views and creating an open environment. Walls may be built 4 to 6 ft. high to create a strong sense of privacy. A low fence with loosely spaced white pickets invites conversation with neighbors, while a tall, dark-stained privacy fence sends a signal that the homeowners prefer to keep to themselves. Similarly, planted boundaries may be low, tall, dense, or loose depending upon their desired impact on the space. A patio surrounded by a colorful, 3-ft.-deep perennial border feels very different from a patio surrounded by a dense, evergreen hedge.

The materials and building methods used for garden walls have a significant impact on the space. Mortared stone walls add weight to a space and give it a sense of having been there forever. Picket fences offer cottage charm. Rose-covered trellises are both classic and romantic in design. And brightly colored concrete walls signal a more contemporary outdoor living area. All can serve as backdrops for planting beds, garden sculpture, and water features.

left · The stone walls on this patio do double duty: They define the boundaries of an outdoor room and serve as a safety feature. The narrow opening for the steps creates a greater sense of enclosure than a broad stairway would, and the flower-filled box planter helps increase the level of privacy.

below · Here, the seat walls are low. They help define boundaries while preserving a very open view and atmosphere. Arbors and fencing along a side, as well as evergreen trees, help screen a neighboring home.

Courtyards with tall masonry walls are often the only way to gain privacy in urban neighborhoods. The canopy of a small tree helps screen views from upstairs rooms of neighboring homes. Softened with plants, courtyards can be captivating spaces.

PUTTING IDEAS ON PAPER

Whether you collaborate with a designer or create your own working plans, it helps to understand the stages of the design process. As you move through this process, it also helps to keep in mind that *more* ideas lead to *better* ideas. Don't settle for first solutions. Instead, play around with many options.

After conducting a site evaluation, designers generally begin the design process with a plot plan of the existing site. You can do this, too, noting the property boundaries and setbacks; any structures that will remain, such as the house, a potting shed, or fences; and important landscape features such as trees. Use tissue paper overlays or make photocopies of your site plan so that you don't have to redraw the plan, and then identify functional spaces and their relationships to each other by drawing a series of loose circles on your site plan. A grilling area might relate both to the indoor kitchen and the outdoor dining area. Open areas for entertaining might connect the living room and an outdoor seating area. A spa might be located in a distant corner or close to the master bedroom for greater privacy.

Next, play around with different patio shapes: rectangular, square, L-shaped (perhaps wrapping around a house corner), circular, or curved. Perhaps the patio will be set on an angle from the house. Divide and conquer—breaking the space into sections with planting beds, containers, or interior walls as dividers. Bump-out sections can also help define functional spaces and add dimension to a patio. If the site is sloped, consider a multilevel terrace.

This is also the time to think about traffic flow and transitions. How might you move from the house to the patio, through the patio, and from the patio to other points in the landscape? If you explore many possibilities, your final plan will likely combine ideas from your various sketches.

Functional Space Plans

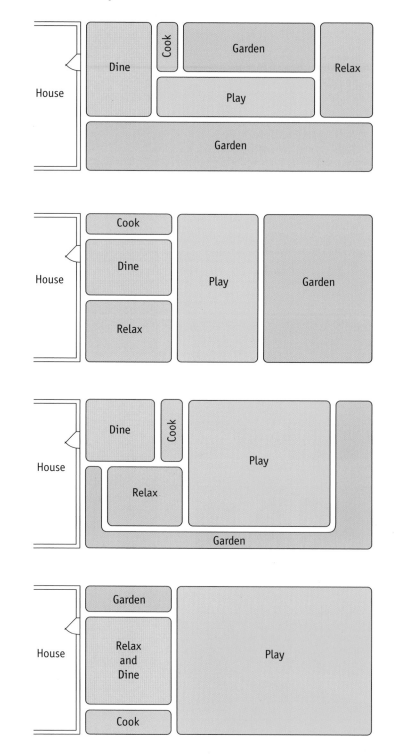

left • This long space could have been straight and narrow, but the gentle curve of the stone retaining wall, which opens up just a bit to give the grill some breathing room, makes this area more inviting. It also helps differentiate the gathering space from the passageway.

below • Very geometric and formal in nature, this sunken patio has a clearly defined seating space. Adding beds of clipped shrubs helps warm the space and give it dimension while also setting the open patio apart from the adjacent covered patio spaces.

Materials with Character

For many, choosing materials is the fun part of the design process. After all, the materials are tangible and have a lot to do with the character of the space. While they may be chosen primarily for aesthetic reasons, it is also important to consider their function, durability, upkeep, and cost. Any good designer will tell you not to skimp on the quality of materials. Although they may cost more initially, quality materials will last longer and age more gracefully.

From an aesthetic standpoint, opt for paving materials that suit the style of your home's architecture and look appropriate in your regional landscape. For instance, Arizona sandstone looks at home in the Southwest, red bricks are common in the South, and bluestone is popular in the Northeast. For formal patios—such as those in front yards or complementing formal architecture and gardens—consider uniform materials such as cut stone, bricks, tile, or pavers that can be laid in a myriad of patterns. Concrete, irregular stone, granite fines, and gravel are ideal for more casual settings. Also, mortared construction gives a more formal or finished appearance than dry-laid construction. Consider combining materials—perhaps adding a band or inset pattern as a focal point in the paving.

Durability varies by material. Granite is much more durable than slate or sandstone. Concrete pavers will withstand freeze-thaw cycles better than poured concrete. Modern brick pavers are much more durable than wall bricks and recycled bricks. In hot climates, tile can be cool underfoot. In wet climates, paving materials with textured surfaces will give better traction, and those made of porous materials or which are dry laid will prevent pooling after a rain. Mortared patios are also easier to maintain than dry laid: They are easier to sweep; materials are less prone to chip, shift, or break; and they don't have to be weeded.

above · Brick is a reasonably priced paving material that is widely available throughout the country. It can be laid in a range of patterns and is equally at home in informal and formal landscapes. Here, it is edged in weathered landscape timbers that add a casual note.

left · These stone slabs contrast with the adjacent gravel even though they are both granite. It's the difference in size and texture that makes them stand out, gives each a unique character, and allows them to be used together.

above · Square pavers have been turned at a 45-degree angle to nearby paving and set amid grass with widely spaced joints to create a well-defined space in the landscape. Although it is adjacent to the pool patio, this space has a sense of being its own small room.

right · Different stones used in different ways make a strong impression. Here, cut flagstone is used both as paving and to construct the seat wall. Slightly rounded cobbles, often reserved for walls or edging, are used as flooring to provide a striking contrast to the neighboring flat, cut stones.

This brick patio was laid in contrasting patterns—herringbone and running bond. This enabled drain grates to be placed more easily near the house while also helping to set apart the seating area. The brick-colored chairs blend right in to the setting.

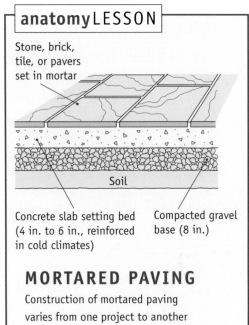

anatomyLESSON

Stone, brick, tile, or pavers set in mortar

Soil

Concrete slab setting bed (4 in. to 6 in., reinforced in cold climates)

Compacted gravel base (8 in.)

MORTARED PAVING

Construction of mortared paving varies from one project to another depending upon climate, soil conditions, techniques, and materials used, but they all have three basic components: a compacted base, a setting bed, and a finished surface.

above · This mortared bluestone patio doesn't require edging to hold the stones in place or to maintain an even surface. The pieces were cut to specification so that they fit neatly together with precisely sized mortared joints.

right · Tile is almost always mortared and set on a solid surface—whether it is used for paving, walls, or outdoor kitchen backsplashes. This helps maintain a smooth surface underfoot and keeps the thin tiles from breaking when pressure is applied.

Paving Materials

The floors of a patio serve both functional and aesthetic roles. They need to be durable in local climates and can help set the tone for an outdoor room. Darker, solid-colored materials will tend to recede visually as a background material, while lighter-colored or mixed materials will attract more attention.

GRAVEL
$

- Range of textures—crushed gravel or pea gravel
- Permeable surface
- Needs to be refreshed every year or two
- Requires weeding
- Snow removal can be difficult
- Can provide uneven surface for furniture

POURED CONCRETE
$

- Available stamped, stained, and with decorative finishes
- Can be made to look like other materials
- Better choice for moderate climates than cold climates

CONCRETE PAVERS
$–$$

- Available in many shapes, sizes, colors, and textures
- Can be mixed, matched, and laid in decorative patterns
- Easily dry laid; can also be mortared
- When dry laid, broken pieces can be replaced
- Permeable pavers available

BRICK
$$

- Available as full-size bricks or thin pavers
- Ideal for traditional architecture
- Can be dry laid or mortared
- When dry laid, broken pieces can be replaced
- Durable
- Can get slippery in damp, shady sites

TILE
$$

- Porcelain and stone tile are ideal for outdoors
- Must be mortared for durability
- Many shapes, sizes, and colors
- Mix and match to create eye-catching patterns
- Durable

STONE
$$–$$$

- Flagstone, cut stone, and granite cobbles
- Can be dry laid or mortared
- When dry laid, it may be possible to replace broken pieces
- Looks natural in the landscape
- Extremely durable

WOOD
$–$$

- Needs to be installed on a frame
- Easy to customize to unusual shapes
- No mortar required
- Choose from rot-resistant woods
- Can be stained and sealed
- Limited long-term durability

above · Cut stone is sold as tile and pavers—the principal difference being the size and thickness. Tiles are generally smaller and thinner and are most often square. They are frequently edged with thicker stone pavers, as they were here. The thicker stone is more durable for pool coping.

far left · Cut flagstone and gravel create two distinctly different patios, with the gravel signaling a more casual atmosphere. Fieldstone was used to build the fire pit and retaining walls, and helps unite the two spaces.

left · Although bricks come in a limited size range, they are available in varied colors and surface textures. These smooth-surfaced bricks were tumbled to soften their edges, providing a weathered look.

STONE

Stone availability varies widely from one part of the country to another. Local stone, which is usually the most economical and readily available, also tends to look the most natural in the landscape. Even so, the range of irregular and cut stone available in stone yards everywhere has increased dramatically in recent years. Prices are often driven by shipping costs (especially for stone imported from other countries). Cost also varies by type, thickness, durability, and by whether the stone has been cut or is irregular—with cut, or "dressed" stone being more expensive.

Stone has a timeless quality that looks at home in almost any environment. Larger pieces of flat stone, whether cut or irregular, are generally referred to as "flagging" or "flagstone." Smaller stones, usually at least somewhat uniform in shape and size, are frequently called "pavers." They include granite cobbles, as well as smoother-surfaced bluestone, granite, and travertine pavers. Even smaller are the different types and sizes of gravel and stone dust—a fine, almost sandy material that comes from crushing rock.

Soft, porous stone, such as sandstone, is suitable for warm, dry climates. In cold climates with freeze-thaw cycles, a dense stone such as bluestone or slate is essential. For paving, seek out flat stones that are easy to walk on, leaving the more rounded and irregular stones for walls and other garden features.

Stone Paving Patterns

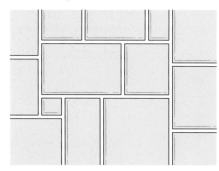

Random with cut pavers

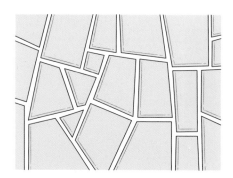

Random with irregular pavers

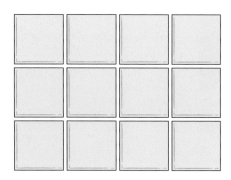

Regular rows with cut pavers of equal size

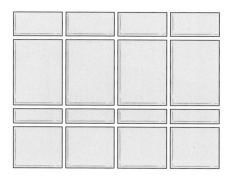

Regular rows with cut pavers of varying sizes

above · These large flagstones were dry-laid with ample space for creeping plants to be tucked into the joints. Such treatment calls for laying the stone flush with the ground level and establishing a secure base so that the stones don't shift or rock underfoot.

right · A field of crushed granite surrounds cut-stone pavers on a rectangular patio in a contemporary landscape. Upright edging laid at the same height as the pavers holds the gravel in position.

far right · Like tile, cut stone can be laid in a range of patterns limited only by your imagination and budget. This eye-catching patio uses small, rectangular cobbles in the joints between cut-stone pavers of random sizes.

BRICK

Paving bricks are formed through a high-firing process that makes them resistant to water absorption, de-icing salts, and breakage; this means they are suitable for cold climates. Most are sold as rectangles in whole and half-brick thicknesses. They come in two standard sizes: Bonded brick pavers are 4 in. by 8 in. for use in dry-laid applications. Modular brick pavers are slightly smaller for use in mortared applications. Many bonded pavers have either chamfered edges or spacer nibs to help prevent edges from chipping. Bricks come in a range of colors, and because the pigmentation is embedded throughout, the colors do not fade. Wall bricks and recycled bricks (which are most often wall bricks) are not of the same density as paving bricks. They will crack and crumble over time, and therefore are not suitable for most paving projects.

Although bricks are sold as rectangles, they can be cut to fit special patterns such as this radiating circle. Here, it is banded by recycled concrete, which was also used to build the retaining wall for the garden beds.

The bricks chosen for this half-circle patio range in color from dark gray to bright red to a very soft, whitish-gray. The light-colored bricks help tie together the light band of paving around the patio and the white trim on the house.

Brick Patterns

Basketweave

Herringbone

Running bond

Stack bond

Brick, when laid in a herringbone pattern, looks good and holds together best with a contrasting "straight" border. Here, that works to safety's advantage, as well. The change in pattern calls attention to the steps.

TILE

Tile is perhaps the most decorative of paving materials and is available in the widest range of colors, shapes, and sizes. Many tiles have patterns that can be mixed and matched to create attractive bands and accents in outdoor flooring. The most durable tile choices for outdoor paving are porcelain and stone—including slate, sandstone, travertine, and granite. Most tiles show minimal wear and can withstand freeze-thaw cycles. Tile is the thinnest of all the paving materials and is typically mortared to prevent cracking and slippage. It is durable and can be chosen to suit a range of architectural styles. Some tiles come as "snap together" pieces to simplify installation.

Stone tile is well-suited for both indoor and outdoor use. On this wide path that leads from a front entry to a parking court, the tile is laid at a 45-degree angle, contrasting with the band of edging and steps.

above • Matching square tiles are laid in a uniform pattern to create a clean, crisp appearance that enables other furnishings to stand out more prominently. The same tile is used in the raised, covered pavilion in the background.

right • Tile is produced both domestically and abroad. The blue tiles embedded in this patio and fountain were purchased by the homeowners during a trip to Spain. They serve as a daily reminder of a special vacation.

CONCRETE

Concrete ranks among the most versatile paving materials. Poured concrete patios can be stamped, stained, etched, or embedded with color and other materials to create a wide range of surfaces—including those that look surprisingly like stone and brick. Poured concrete is most suitable for warm climates.

Concrete pavers, by contrast, are dense products made to withstand freeze-thaw cycles and de-icing salts common in cold climates. They come in a wide range of shapes, sizes, colors, and textures and can be mixed and matched or laid in an infinite range of running, modular, or random patterns for a durable and decorative patio surface. Many look like brick or stone and some are permeable, allowing water to soak through. Although most have a lifespan of 30 years or more, over time they can wear slightly, resulting in a somewhat faded look. They are moderately priced and easy to install and maintain.

Poured concrete was embedded with small pea gravel to create a pad and several oversized pavers in this narrow yard. The patio is just slightly wider than the path, but it provides enough room for a couple of chairs.

Concrete Paver Patterns

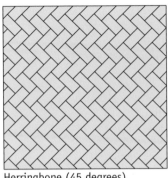

Herringbone (45 degrees)

Herringbone (90 degrees)

Running bond

Basketweave

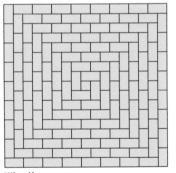

Whorling square

Basketweave variation

Pattern with squares

above • The earth-colored concrete pavers were laid on angle with the swimming pool and banded with cut gray stone near the pool's coping, or edge. The color blends comfortably with the stone pillars and stucco walls.

left • Poured concrete can be easily shaped into free-formed patios. Here, it provides seamless coping around a swimming pool and the partially buried boulders at the pool's edge. Joints in the concrete allow it to expand and contract with temperature and moisture changes.

WOOD

Although wood flooring is beautiful outdoors, its use is most often reserved for decking. It can also be used for patios, with wooden tiles and slats laid directly over a concrete patio, well-compacted gravel, or other existing surface for an updated look. Because many wood tiles lock together, they can be easily laid without tools, nails, or adhesive. Teak, rosewood, ipé, and composite deck tiles (generally made from a mix of plastic, wood, and other materials) are all excellent choices that offer varying degrees of rot resistance and lasting beauty. Even so, when used in an outdoor application, wood is still less durable than stone or masonry products. Depending upon their density and installation method, expect 5 to 15 years from most wood paving products. Wood rounds—slices or cross-sections of tree trunks—can also be set in sand to create an eye-catching mosaic paving pattern.

left · Wood is among the easiest materials to work with when it comes to custom shapes because it is so easy to cut. Here, one section is laid at an angle to another. In addition, both sections wrap around curved sections of stone.

above • Wood combines beautifully with other materials, as it does here with small river cobbles and concrete paving. With the step laid at a contrasting angle, the design varied the pattern and was able to call attention to the grade change.

Mix and Match Materials

Something as simple as a band of contrasting paving materials can give a patio just the right pizzazz. And the opportunities for mixing and matching paving materials are endless. Whether creating a mortared or dry-laid patio, materials of contrasting shape, size, texture, and color can be mixed and matched to create a variety of patterns and mosaics to add visual interest to outdoor flooring.

1. Small, cut stones have been combined with larger, irregular flagstone pavers and small, black cobbles for a unique design. The cut stones are laid so that they gently slope from the patio into a shallow water feature. 2. Rather than pave the entire patio in cut bluestone, the designer replaced segments with rounded cobbles for a striking effect. The inner edge of the patio is laid "ragged," and creeping plants are encouraged to soften the edges of the paving. 3. By laying gray river cobbles in a geometric pattern among crushed stone of a lighter, contrasting color, the designer has created a very formal "room within a room." Perfect squares and circles, both used in this design, are the most formal shapes in a garden. 4. Brick and bluestone are common companions that are especially suited to traditional homes up and down the East Coast. Often, one serves as a edging for the other, but here the brick is used to create bold visual joints between the square stone pavers.

PATIOS FOR

Patios can be a welcoming entry courtyard,

a dining patio beyond the kitchen,

EVERY

or a poolside patio out back. Each serves a unique role

that meets the needs of homeowners.

PURPOSE

While most often relegated to the backyard, patios can be placed just about anywhere in the landscape and serve a range of purposes. They can welcome guests to your home, provide a place to cook and dine, afford a quiet escape, or offer a gathering place for friends and family in the garden or around a pool. They extend your home's livable space outdoors—creating destinations just beyond your living room, kitchen, or bedroom door as well as in more distant locations in the landscape. Indeed, a series of outdoor patios can surround a home in much the same way a deck can wrap around a house—offering access from any room. Patios can also vary in size from an intimate patio for two just beyond the master bedroom to an expansive patio beyond the living room for hosting large gatherings of family and friends.

Patios may be open to views, enclosed for a greater sense of privacy or, most likely, some combination of the two. After all, part of the joy of being outdoors is being able to take in the surrounding landscape, so what may be needed is "just enough" privacy and screening from unwanted views. Patios may be very simple in nature, using only a minimum of materials, or highly styled with features such as outdoor kitchens, hearths, water features, and walls. What matters is how you plan to use the space.

When designing a patio, think about its purpose. If it is adjacent to a room in the house, consider ways in which the patio can serve as an extension of that space. If you have a specific goal in mind for a patio, consider where it might be best placed. How many people will use the space? How will they use it? What time of day or even in what season will they enjoy it most? The answers to these questions will help shape the space—its size, sense of openness or enclosure, and its features, such as seating, lighting, or overhead cover.

above · Often, the best or most interesting views are from the front of the house—so why not enjoy them? By expanding the front door landing and adding a few chairs, these homeowners have created both a welcoming entry and a place to sit and relax.

right · Installing a bar—with or without stools—is a practical and convenient strategy for homeowners who entertain frequently. The overhead light above this bar provides ample illumination for the bartender after dark.

above · Patios that extend at grade level from a living room are ideal for entertaining—whether that means tea with a special friend or hosting a larger gathering for a cocktail party. This patio is cozy and inviting, comfortable enough for two, but with standing room for many.

left · By introducing a grade change in an otherwise flat landscape, the designer was able to add visual interest in this small backyard, which overlooks a golf course. It also clearly defines the space designated for cooking and dining.

Welcoming Front Entry Patios

Front entries are the gateway to a home. They are where visitors are welcomed and signal what is to be expected beyond—both inside and outside a home. As such, they should be clearly identifiable, easily traversed, and carefully maintained. Broad steps and a generous landing will help create a strong sense of arrival.

Front-yard patios are most often designed as transitional spaces used for greeting guests and seeing them off at the end of a visit. They are places to linger, not necessarily to cook and entertain. For this reason, they are usually smaller than backyard patios, taking the form of stoops and landings. But they can be much more than that, and a broad entry with a trickling water feature, an arbor covered with fragrant vines, or some simple seating will provide an enjoyable experience for all. In some neighborhoods, front patios function much like front porches—providing a comfortable place to sit for a while, visiting with passersby, and creating a neighborly environment. Entry courtyards, because of the privacy created by their walls, can often be used for entertaining, as well. And on some city lots, it's the only space available for outdoor living.

Because homeowners and their guests come and go at all hours, good lighting is essential. If possible, there should be space to discreetly leave packages and to stand out of the rain. Pathways leading to the front patio should be wider than those elsewhere in the landscape, allowing for two people to walk side by side.

above · **A bench placed just beyond the front door is a sign of welcome. It also serves practical purposes—a place to sit and read the mail, remove muddy shoes, or leave packages out of the rain.**

above · Set close to the street, this front patio is neighborhood-friendly. The grade change and wall help establish some boundaries and create a sense of intimacy, but it is still easy to visit with neighbors who are out for an evening walk.

left · This small, brick patio has been designed as a cozy nook. The low, clipped hedge defines the room's boundaries, and small trees offer a bit of shade and screening. The side positioning of the bench signals that this is more of a casual gathering area than a place for observing neighborhood happenings.

far left · Roof overhangs don't have to be large. This arch-style overhang is primarily decorative, and it provides just enough cover to duck out of the rain, if needed. The brick patio functions much as a covered porch would on other homes.

Patios for Every Purpose 63

An Entry Courtyard

For homes built amid a broad, rolling plain of low-growing piñons, junipers, native grasses, and wildflowers, attached courtyards often provide the only outdoor refuge from the beautiful, yet spare, native landscape. So when redesigning the entry for this home, Clemens & Associates created a new courtyard to do just that.

The original entry had a narrow, copper-flashed "eyebrow" that provided limited protection for guests and the front door itself during infrequent, but sometimes-heavy rainstorms. A front-entry makeover that included a custom front door, a covered entry, and a courtyard garden solved the water issue, created a warm and inviting space, and better connected the home to the landscape. The new courtyard entry also buffers the home's entrance from the parking area, driveway, and street.

Working with mass and geometry were important design aspects of the project. They keep the entrance in scale and style with the home. The new, deep roof overhang sits atop a large, powder-coated, steel column that has an attached collar and carrier beam to give the illusion that the roof mass is floating around the column. Natural light shining in through this collar, as well as through two skylights, helps illuminate the covered entry.

The exterior walls reflect the circular and angular geometry of the home, and the grid pattern of an iron gate echoes the pattern in the new front door. There are a small patio for a table and chairs, raised-bed planting areas, and a sheet waterfall built into an Anasazi-style stacked-stone wall. The textured stonework set against the flat stucco wall turns the water feature into a focal point of the entry, while the falling water helps set the tone for a pleasant visit.

Rectilinear steps replaced the original "wedding cake" steps, and an architectural pedestal supports a large, decorative container. The roof extension, which features a pair of skylights, is supported by a powder-coated, steel post. The stone wall features a mortared veneer of Arizona rose stone and a sheet waterfall.

The square grid in the iron gate mirrors the grid in the front door. The gate's rusty patina is echoed in the wall light fixture and picks up the coloring in the moss rock used to create the raised planting beds.

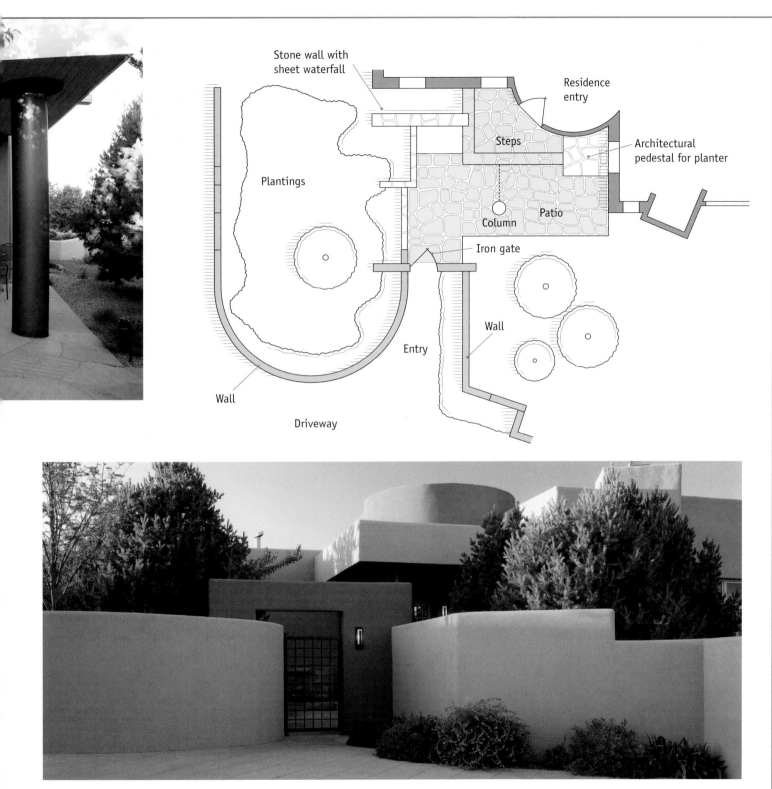

Stone wall with
sheet waterfall

Residence
entry

Steps

Architectural
pedestal for planter

Plantings

Patio

Column

Iron gate

Wall

Entry

Wall

Driveway

The combination of curved and angular walls echoes elements from the home's architecture. They also
help to visually bring the house down to ground level, providing a stronger connection to the surrounding
rolling plains. Contrasting stucco colors provide visual interest and help call attention to the entry gate.

Cozy Backyard Patios

On a small lot, there may not be room for a large patio. But even on large lots, small patios are often the most inviting. Low seating walls or perennial borders around the periphery of a small patio can make it cozy without feeling claustrophobic. Trickling water features are especially appreciated in cozy spaces and help create a calm setting in urban neighborhoods, where space for outdoor living is limited.

Interestingly, one of the best ways to make a modest space feel larger is to divide it into two or three cozy spaces. This divide-and-conquer strategy also works to make large lots more manageable and intimate. One of the nicest aspects of a smaller, more manageable space is the ability to pay attention to details—opting for quality over quantity. Unique furniture finds are more affordable when you only need a few of them. Gardens are easier to maintain when they are limited to containers or small beds with favorite plants.

Cozy spaces are often quiet spaces surrounded by soothing green foliage. But there are no rules against making them colorful, invigorating spaces if that better suits your personality and style. Focus on creating an inviting space that makes you feel good and showcases the things you love.

Patios tucked just outside a bedroom are especially inviting as places to greet the day or to relax before retiring for the evening. This small brick patio is simply designed, with two comfortable armchairs that share an ottoman. A path provides easy access to other points in the landscape.

above · Rustic charm oozes from this small patio. It was built against the house and takes up minimal space—thereby capitalizing on every square inch of the compact yard for roses, delphiniums, irises, and other favorite perennials.

left · This small patio belongs to a condominium owner. The bar-style table and stools provide a spot for tea or a light meal and offer a view of the neighboring golf course. The irregular pattern of the patio's edge adds visual interest.

above · These homeowners love bright colors and bold design, yet the space is still simply designed. The Adirondack chairs have a deep, slanted seat that signals it's time to settle down and unwind. Their broad arms offer a place to rest a book or drink.

Patios for Cooking and Dining

Patios have always provided a place to grill hot dogs and host picnics. Backyard grilling has become easier and more appealing than ever before with the introduction of grills with enhanced features, grilling islands with counter space, and fully equipped outdoor kitchens.

Multiple cooking surfaces with separate temperature controls have made it possible to cook an entire meal outdoors, while countertops and sinks have simplified food preparation and serving. Outdoor refrigerators keep drinks cold and allow ingredients to be kept fresh and readily available, while cabinets provide convenient storage for cooking and serving pieces. Even so, most patios for cooking are located just beyond the home's kitchen for convenience and cleanup. Close proximity to the house also means easier access to water, power, and gas lines.

Just as important as the cooking area is the dining area—whether a pull-up bar, an extension of the grilling island, or a separate dining table with chairs. Comfortable and stylish furnishings—from classic teak tables to quaint bistro sets—turn dining beneath the stars into all-evening affairs. Umbrellas, awnings, and pavilions can provide protection from sun and rain. And outdoor lighting—in addition to helping you see what you are cooking and eating—can be used to create ambience.

above · This patio features an outdoor kitchen with sink, wood-burning pizza oven, and wood storage units. The rustic dining pavilion provides shade in the sunny California climate. And two oversized, camp-style picnic tables provide ample seating for the family and friends.

right · The grilling cabinet on this compact patio doubles as a wall, while the arbor provides screening overhead. Painting or staining the arbor a light color, keeping the vines trimmed so that they don't get too dense, and accenting the patio with flowers help keep the space bright.

Close proximity of the grilling and dining areas to the kitchen simplifies serving and cleanup for these homeowners. Double doors that open onto the patio with a minimal grade change also make it easier for carrying dishes back and forth.

Gathering Spaces

Patios are ideal gathering places for family and friends. The size of a patio and how it is furnished depends upon how many people will gather there on a regular basis and what kind of atmosphere you wish to create. If the goal is a place to settle into for the evening, comfortable furniture is a must—whether deep-seated Adirondack chairs or plush, cushioned sofas and side chairs. An assortment of small tables offers a place to set down drinks and reading materials, as well as to play games or display favorite objects.

To accommodate gatherings of different sizes, consider incorporating low walls around a patio that can double as additional seating when you have extra guests. Another strategy is to develop a series of adjacent outdoor rooms or patios that can be used during parties. This allows guests to either join in the main discussion or venture off with a few others for a more intimate conversation.

Outdoor hearths can also enhance a gathering space—both warming things up on a chilly evening and providing a focal point in an outdoor room. A nearby outdoor kitchen or freestanding grill will make serving snacks a snap, and a refrigerator stocked with beverages will limit the treks back indoors. Also, don't forget to wire your patio for outdoor sound. Stereo systems with multiple output channels and weatherproof speakers are ideal. Even television sets have become popular for watching favorite shows or movies.

One of the easiest ways to provide shade for a gathering is with a large market umbrella. This one rests on a stand and can be moved when needed as the sun shifts in the sky. Sturdy teak chairs are softened with cushions and accented with colorful pillows.

above · Few things are more enjoyable than relaxing around the hearth with friends. Doing so outdoors takes the experience to a whole new level. Although heat tends to dissipate quickly outdoors, both the retaining wall and the close proximity of seating to the fireplace help ensure that guests stay warm on a cool evening.

left · This patio was designed specifically for gathering (rather than dining or cooking) and with a specific number of people in mind. The six chairs fit the space just right, with adequate room for passage on all sides.

Spacious Patios for Entertaining

If entertaining crowds is something you enjoy, a more spacious patio may best fit your needs. Broad, open patios built at the same level as the house and which extend from a family or living room can create an almost seamless indoor-outdoor environment for entertaining. Building a multilevel patio on a hillside can create a sense of intrigue that compels guests to move farther into the landscape.

Large spaces open to views of the landscape are well-suited to entertaining larger crowds. In more urban or suburban settings, providing loose screening as well as overhead structures such as pergolas and pavilions will offer a greater sense of privacy.

To visually anchor a spacious patio, be sure to include trees and shrubs in adjacent borders. They can be used to create vignettes, provide shade and screening, and make a more natural transition to the landscape beyond. Also consider creating a series of seating and gathering areas on a broad patio to make it feel more intimate when used by just a few individuals at a time.

right · This home, patio, and lawn were all built on the same grade, making for an easy transition between indoors and out. Because the patio stretches across the back of the house, it can be accessed from several doors, which greatly enhances traffic flow during a large gathering.

facing page top · This bluestone patio features multiple seating areas and plenty of room for activities or mingling during parties. The table can easily seat six to eight, while the chairs gathered around a portable fire pit create a casual conversation area.

facing page bottom · Although the grade changes are minimal, the multilevel design of this broad patio distinguishes separate areas for different activities. In addition to those shown for dining and gathering around the fire, there is an outdoor kitchen, small swimming pool with its own patio, and a covered patio near the back door.

Sheltered Patios

Covered patios—those with solid roofs overhead—come in three principal forms: Those recessed into a house such as a portico, arcade, portal, or loggia; those extending from a house with a roof or arbor overhead; and freestanding patios with pavilions, pergolas, or other roofed structures overhead. They provide essential protection from the elements in climates where rainfall is frequent or the summer sun can be brutal, and they can offer an inviting outdoor environment in any region.

Recessed patios—whether they run the length of a house or are tucked into a corner by a door—should be at least 6 ft. deep to accommodate both a sitting area and passage. Larger homes often have porticos or loggias that are 8 to 10 ft. deep and offer greater variety when it comes to arranging furniture. Covered patios that extend from a house come in a wider range of shapes and sizes—often deeper and squarish in shape. Like their attached cousins, freestanding covered patios may be built at or above grade level and are often open on all sides.

Sheltered patios can accommodate a full range of outdoor living amenities and benefit from landscaping. They are especially suitable for container plantings and vines that can scramble up their columns and posts.

top right · This partially enclosed breezeway doubles as patio for dining, while the grid of square pavers expands the usable space beyond the sheltered patio. The yellow-painted walls and windows help create a bright, light-filled space.

right · This roofed patio extends from the house, creating a cozy nook. The lattice along the back wall creates a sense of enclosure without blocking views of the rear garden or hampering air circulation. A rustic twig chandelier hangs from the vaulted, beamed ceiling.

facing page · Porticos such as this one commonly feature high ceilings and columns. Their open nature—and in this case, the ceiling fans, too—ensures good air circulation, even though the space is covered. This one is adjacent to a series of French doors that provide access to different rooms of the home.

Patio and Deck Combos

A deck and patio combination is a great solution for sloping sites. It adds three-dimensional visual interest, helps ease the transition from the house to the landscape, and tends to make good use of the topography. It can also double or triple the amount of available outdoor living space and allow for a variety of outdoor environments since each space can be designated for a different use. For instance, the deck may be geared toward cooking and dining, while the patio offers a more casual or romantic ambience for relaxing well into the evening.

Transitions are an important aspect of a deck and patio combination. Just a few broad steps will make them feel more united, while narrow or winding steps will call attention to their separate identities. They may be connected with wooden steps that match the deck, masonry steps that match the patio, or contrasting steps that distinctly define a transition. Stairs or multiple runs of steps with landings may be needed on steep lots, and a spiral staircase may provide a compact solution on tight lots or where the patio is located beneath the deck. Landscaping can help tie together the deck and patio visually. Boulders and plantings can also help to secure the slope, preventing erosion. And for safety, don't forget landscape lighting—whether step lights attached to the railing, path lights at the bottom of the steps, or overhead lights that help illuminate the entire area.

above · Both the deck and patio of this home sport a contemporary look with clean lines, which are accented by the single row of ornamental grasses and low stone wall. The steps lead to an infinity edge pool, with views of the surrounding Cascade Mountains.

right · The wood used on the far deck was repeated on the near patio beneath a spa, providing a sense of continuity in the landscape. The stone patio in between feels equally at home in the rocky terrain.

left · This deck and patio combination provides a variety of gathering and dining spaces—including a special place for the kids. The earthy tones in the wood and brick complement each other, while the solid risers on the steps and the lower walls of the deck give a finished look to the space.

Spacious Deck and Patio Combo

When Alexander and Janet Patterson first contacted the Fockele Garden Company, they had two goals in mind: To resolve a drainage problem that plagued their backyard lawn and to create an inviting seating area that was flexible enough to accommodate an evening with friends or just the two of them alone. The result is a gracious "sunken" bluestone patio that creates an experience of "being within a garden."

The bluestone is mortared in place, but not between the joints. This creates a permeable surface that allows rainwater to drain into a gravel chamber below. Other runoff on the property is directed here as well, and a series of perforated pipes distributes the water underground. An overflow pipe carries excess water to a nearby rain garden—a depressed area in the woodland garden in which moisture-loving plants grow while the collected water slowly settles into the soil.

An existing retaining wall that was part brick and part stone was reworked—replacing the stone with used brick that was sourced from four locations and then whitewashed with a thin layer of mortar to give them a similar appearance to the bricks in the existing wall. The semicircular section of the wall was added as well, creating a raised bed and a strong focal point from both the deck and home. Lush container plantings flank the corners of the terrace, and a woodland path leads visitors to an adjacent sculpture garden. Bamboo and a dense semicircle of emerald arborvitae were planted for screening. Together, the deck, terrace, and gardens reflect the Pattersons' love of art, nature, and family.

top · In addition to seating and dining areas on the deck, three additional seating areas on the patio give the homeowners plenty of options for gathering outdoors. This bistro table is ideal for morning coffee or a romantic dinner for two. A nearby table has seating for four, and the deck has a table for six. For larger gatherings, all of the tables can be used.

right · The patio served as the solution to a drainage problem. Pavers are mortared onto a gravel base but not between the joints, so water drains into a gravel chamber beneath the patio and is distributed through a series of perforated pipes. An overflow pipe running to the adjacent woodland garden helps out in heavy rains.

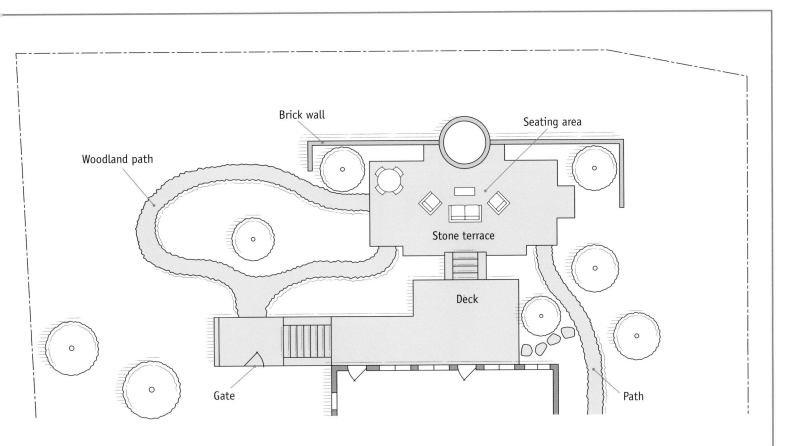

Brick wall

Woodland path

Seating area

Stone terrace

Deck

Gate

Path

left · The view from the deck is an inviting one. Bamboo and an arborvitae hedge screen neighboring houses, while the large pot serves as a focal point. Teak chairs and benches offer a comfortable place to gather.

Balconies and Rooftops

Balcony and rooftop patios are growing in popularity not only in cities, but in other geographic locations as well. Balconies, especially, suit a wide range of home styles. They may have a very small footprint or run the length of a home. Rooftop patios are welcome additions to homes with a flat roof—common not only to high-rise buildings, but also to architectural styles such as those found in the Southwest.

Before embarking on a rooftop or balcony project, it is important to know local codes and to establish the weight-bearing capacity of the structure. Paving materials, soil, plants, water, furniture, and other elements can be heavy. You also need to make sure you have a way to get these items up there, as carrying soil through living spaces can be messy and hauling construction materials up steps can be difficult. Once you have logistics, safety issues, and any building inspector issues out of the way, the fun begins.

Balconies and rooftops are like any other patio space, but they require a bit more ingenuity. For instance, striking the right balance on weight is important: Containers and furnishings should be light enough to minimize weight, but heavy enough not to blow over easily. Small items that might topple in a storm should be avoided, and small trees should be securely anchored. Container plantings are a mainstay on balconies and rooftops and can be arranged for accent or to create the impression of a lush garden setting. They can be used to frame or screen views, or to serve as living "walls" to create separate "rooms" and to bring the space to life. Box planters, which can hold a lot of plants yet aren't too heavy, are especially practical.

above • This city balcony is paved in tile and filled with lush foliage you'd expect to find in spacious landscapes. Ornamental grasses, small trees, hydrangeas, and shrubby dogwoods fill dark-colored box planters and round pots, creating a secluded getaway high above the treetops.

facing page top • Flat-roofed homes can be ideal for terraces—provided they are rated to handle the weight. Rooftop (left) and balcony (right) patios adjoin this Santa Fe home, providing views of the distant Sangre de Christo Mountains.

facing page bottom • Low box planters and an open railing help preserve views from this balcony as well as from the adjacent room. Pots filled with bamboo help anchor the corners of this contemporary urban space.

Wood is also a lightweight option for flooring, although other materials can be more durable. Light-colored paving is a good option because it reflects rather than absorbs heat. Arbors can also sometimes be built on a rooftop if they meet local codes. As with any space, the key is working with the space, views, and challenges they present. Sometimes, the more challenging the space, the more creative the solutions.

Terraced Hillsides

Although the terms patio and terrace are often used inter-changeably, a terrace refers specifically to a paved surface that has been carved out of a slope, usually through a process of cut and fill, in which earth from above is moved below to create a level area. As a result, terraces often have retaining walls built into their upper sides and may have freestanding walls on their lower sides.

Terraces may comprise a single patio area or multiple, connected spaces. Depending upon the slope, one may step directly from one terrace onto another, traverse a series of connecting steps, or follow along a gradually sloping path to reach the next terrace. Each type of transition creates a very different experience, with the first being more architectural in nature and the last being more about a contemplative journey through the landscape. A series of terraces can be designed to highlight a property's unique features—shaded areas, special views, natural rock outcroppings, or other elements.

above · This brick-edged, stone patio sits just beneath a second, raised patio that is located beyond the back door. The path on the left wends its way to a third, much smaller patio in the garden below. A mix of in-ground gardens and container plantings surround the main patio without blocking views.

above · On steep sites such as this California hillside, it is often possible to create a series of gathering spaces connected by steps. The upper patio features a wall and steps built from recycled concrete. The lower patio includes an outdoor kitchen and dining area.

right • Hardscaping was kept to a minimum on this steep, woodland hillside. Four of the five small patios, all positioned on different levels, are shown in this photo. Winding mulched paths and stone steps lead from one space to another on their way to the lake.

below • A level patio was carved out of this hillside adjacent to the house. A tall retaining wall holds back the bank on the upper side, while dense plantings and steps made from large stones control erosion on the lower side.

Poolside Patios

Poolside patios are seasonal favorites—popular destinations in warm weather, used when sunning, swimming, and gathering with friends. And they can include full-service amenities such as outdoor hearths, outdoor kitchens, and an assortment of comfortable furniture.

As when designing any patio, consider both circulation patterns and gathering spaces. A pool deck with a depth of 10 to 12 ft. can accommodate a row of chaises and still provide space for passage. A deeper poolside patio will offer greater flexibility when it comes to selecting and arranging furniture.

Paving materials should be safe to walk on, even when wet. That means both a nonskid surface and something cooler underfoot. Dark surfaces absorb heat, while light surfaces and those topped with an acrylic coating tend to be cooler. Lightly textured surfaces are less likely to result in slippage when wet. And mortared stone, brick, tile, or pavers with flat surfaces will minimize tripping and stubbed toes.

A shade structure—whether a pool house, pavilion, or pergola—can provide a much-needed escape from sweltering heat and sun. A fan overhead will help cool things off and keep the bugs at bay. If the pool and patio are located at a distance from the home, including an undercounter refrigerator for drinks in the grilling island or outdoor kitchen will reduce trips back to the house.

Even if you opt to keep things simple, consider how you'll transport and store pool supplies, food and beverages, and items such as seat cushions or pool floats. Pathways that are wide and smooth enough for rolling coolers or carts will make the trip easier, and onsite storage bins can prove indispensable.

top • Pool patios don't have to be large. There is plenty of space on this small poolside patio to eat lunch, relax in the spa, or dry off after a few laps in the pool. A steppingstone path leads back to the house.

above • A strong sense of continuity is created when the same paving materials that surround the pool extend beneath this covered patio. Minimalist styling and soft, natural colors help turn this into a serene setting for swimming, relaxing, or visiting with friends.

left · The irregular shape, change in levels, sheet waterfalls, contrasting tile colors, and extra stone lip around the pool's edge all add visual interest to this corner patio. The pool features several small patios; this one is located just beyond the master bedroom.

below · The curve of this pool and patio echoes the curve of the home and arbor. Lounge chairs overlook the infinity edge pool and view, while a dining table is located near an outdoor kitchen alcove. Boulders at the pool's edge help tie everything into the native landscape.

A Poolside Patio

Summers are especially long and hot in the Hill Country of southern Texas, where it's not uncommon for temperatures to soar above 100°F six months of the year. Swimming pools are a welcome sight and a common element in the landscape. The white limestone used around this pool and patio reflect rather than absorb the sun's rays, also helping to keep things a few degrees cooler, while two sturdy arbors create a bit of shade.

Designed by Da Vida Pools, this custom pool and its surrounding patios were built on a slope that drops off from a flat, upper lawn area. There is no need for a diving board, as those who like to make a splash can simply jump into the pool from the upper deck. A level entry is provided from an intermediate-level poolside patio closer to the house. There are also steps leading up to the pool from a lower pathway, where the swimming pool cascades into a small basin, creating a water feature in the garden. Other special features of the pool include two sheet waterfalls and a swim-up bar with underwater stools near the grill.

Three patios surround this pool. The lower patio is mostly for access and convenience to the house, where there is a screened-in porch to offer additional shelter and protection from flying insects. The larger, upper patio is the main gathering space for dining, relaxing, and entertaining. It features a fire pit for winter use, high-top table seating, an arbor, and bar seating. On the back side of the main patio, steps lead to a small, lower patio devoted to cooking.

top · A long, narrow bar was built along the back side of the patio for seating and serving. Without stools, it works especially well for a cocktail party where seating isn't necessary, yet it is nice to be able to set down a plate. The bar is also a convenient place to study or work on a sunny afternoon.

right · The pool features a swim-up bar with built-in underwater stools near the outdoor kitchen. Constructed from local Texas limestone, the retaining walls around the pool deck feature sheet waterfalls for their sound and beauty.

left · The pool and patio were built on a slope, with the pool located several feet below the main patio grade. The patio includes a fire pit, arbor, bar, and seating area. A hammock hangs beneath the arbor.

above · The outdoor kitchen is located on the far side of the patio, down steps and beneath a wisteria-covered arbor. In addition to a gas grill, the grilling cabinet includes a side burner and ample storage space.

Enclosed Courtyards

Courtyards can provide both a sense of privacy and protection from the elements. Walls screen unwanted views and provide a windbreak while creating a backdrop for plantings, outdoor kitchens, and garden elements.

Although most courtyards feature masonry walls, they can be enclosed with a variety of materials— some very solid, others providing only loose screening. Courtyard walls can also vary in height. Low seat walls, for instance, clearly define a courtyard's boundaries in a friendly, inviting way. Tall, solid masonry walls declare a desire for privacy, yet can be opened up with "windows" or cutouts placed in both the walls and gates. Fence boards can be fit tightly together or be spaced loosely apart—thus affecting both air flow and views.

An arbor adds immensely to the sense of enclosure, but is usually best if it covers only a portion of the courtyard. After all, among the reasons for spending time outdoors are to enjoy the natural light and to feel connected to the surrounding landscape. Entry arches and gates can add much to the personality of a space. Plantings—whether in beds or pockets at ground level, in raised beds, or in containers—help soften the many hard surfaces typically found in a courtyard and absorb sound that might otherwise echo in the space. They warm up a courtyard, making it feel more inviting.

above • It can be a challenge to create privacy outdoors in the city. Tall brick walls topped by lattice help do the trick here. Adding planting pockets around the edges and extending out into the patio for vines, small ornamental trees, and other small plants helps soften the space and create textural interest. A long bench increases seating capacity.

above • This small courtyard is surrounded by four walls but open to the sky two stories overhead. Glass doors on two walls both provide access to the patio and offer garden views from multiple rooms of this urban house.

The window in this high, stucco wall creates a sense of intrigue, brightens the space, serves as a focal point, and makes this outdoor room feel surprisingly like an indoor room—even though it is covered in plants. The choice and place of furniture also add to the feeling.

Destination Patios

On large lots and those with distant views, it is common to create a destination patio closer to the property's edge. But destination patios—those not adjacent to the house—can be a fun addition to small properties, as well. They can provide a unique backyard getaway and be used for gathering for any purpose. Younger family members, especially, may appreciate having their own place to hang out with friends out of earshot of parents.

Think about whether or not you wish to be able to view it from the house, and what kind of experience you wish to create on your journey to the destination patio. Is it easily viewed and clearly inviting or are you more interested in creating a sense of intrigue by screening it from view and laying a winding path?

Destination patios can also adjoin outbuildings— whether a backyard studio, pool house, guest house, or garden shed. Freestanding patios are frequently adorned with gazebos, pergolas, or pavilions. If you plan to use the destination patio for cooking and dining, be sure to consider convenience issues when designing outdoor kitchens. The better furnished the space, the fewer trips you'll need to make carrying supplies to and from the house.

top · This small patio, featuring a spa and outdoor shower, is located just off the main patio, where it has been lightly screened for an increased sense of privacy. The rectangular shape and smooth surface of the spa patio contrast sharply with the round, pebbled-concrete main patio.

right · Small patios can be tucked into nooks and crannies throughout a landscape. Woodland gardens, such as this one, are especially amenable to the creation of quiet destination patios. The low, stacked-stone wall lends a sense of permanence and age to the setting.

above • The above-grade patio was positioned where you would normally expect a raised garden bed. As such, it is especially intriguing and offers a different perspective on the landscape for those who gather there.

left • Red ranks among the most compelling colors in any landscape. These red chairs, set amid a circle of trees and hedges, catch the eye from a distance, beckoning guests to the round patio even though it is located away from the house.

WALLS

Walls can be low or tall, dense or airy.

Ceilings can be shady, solid, or open to the sky.

AND SHADE

Together, they define the atmosphere of an

outdoor room more than any other element.

STRUCTURES

Walls, Fences, and Screening

Walls, fences, and dense screening can be used to create enclosed spaces, define patio boundaries, buffer noise and wind, screen unwanted views, and frame desirable views. Retaining walls help hold soil in place and can provide an attractive backdrop for plantings, water features, and garden sculpture. Low walls can double as seating areas, making an outdoor space both more functional and adaptable. The density and height of a wall or fence send a message to neighbors and passersby about how you wish to relate to them. Low, open fences are commonly viewed as a sign of welcome. Tall, dense walls clearly signal that you appreciate your privacy.

Mortared walls may be made from brick, stone, poured concrete, or stucco. Stone walls can be dry laid or mortared, depending upon their height and the materials used. Brick walls can be solid or open-weave. Stucco walls can be finished in an infinite variety of colors and textures to match a home or the color scheme in a garden.

Fences provide an affordable alternative to walls when it comes to screening and privacy. They come in a range of materials from natural, stained, and painted wood to an assortment of metals. Like walls, they can be low or high, and their boards or pickets may be either widely or tightly spaced depending upon their purpose. Hedges and dense mixed plantings also offer an attractive and affordable alternative for screening, although it may take time for them to grow in.

Before you begin construction on walls and fences, be sure to check local building codes and homeowner association requirements that might dictate their height, minimum distance from property boundaries or street curbs, and placement regarding utilities. Although less common, some communities may also have guidelines regarding hedges.

above · Relatively flat stones are easier to work with when building a stacked-stone wall like this one, even when they vary greatly in thickness. The broad, thick capstones running across the top were rough-cut with chiseled edges to fit.

left · This low, curving, stone wall creates an attractive boundary and safety feature. It has been mortared for stability, although the mortar has been removed from the edges so that it appears to be a dry-stack wall.

facing page top · Wooden walls don't have to be fences. Sometimes they are simply walls, like these tongue-and-groove paneled walls that frame a covered patio on one side of a garage. Open at the top for light and airflow, these walls provide privacy and help protect the space on a rainy or windy day.

facing page bottom · The large, framed window in this tall masonry wall has an iron grid but no panes. It provides views out, as well as intimate glimpses into this brick courtyard. The wall also serves as a solid backdrop for plants such as lavender and bougainvillea.

FREESTANDING WALLS

In addition to creating privacy and defining boundaries, freestanding walls can also be used to divide spaces and direct the flow of traffic. Walls can block access to an area, while their openings—often marked with gates, arches, or transitional arbors—clearly define passageways. Walls also create microclimates for plantings by screening wind, absorbing the sun's heat, or casting deep shade. In many cases, this protected environment enables gardeners to grow plants that might not otherwise survive in their climate.

Freestanding, dry-laid stone walls are common in New England and other regions. They are typically built with native stone set on a solid footing just below grade level and are held together by friction and gravity. They taper inward toward the top, which is usually finished with a layer of capstones. Well-proportioned stone walls typically measure 2 ft. wide by 3 ft. high or 3 ft. wide by 4 ft. high. Gabion walls—strong wire cages filled with loose stones—offer another approach to creating a freestanding stone wall.

Mortared stone walls must be built on a solid, concrete foundation, but a wider variety of stone can be used in their construction and the stones need not fit together quite so neatly, as gaps can be filled with mortar. They can be made to look like dry-laid walls by "raking" out the mortar along the face of the stone before it dries. Brick, poured concrete, concrete block, and stucco walls are more affordable and popular alternatives to stone that offer a variety of finishes. Also, materials can be mixed and matched—perhaps pillars and coping that contrast with wall materials—for dramatic effect.

above · This mortared retaining wall was built at sitting height, providing a place to pause overlooking the pool. It is also being put to good use as a pedestal supporting planted containers and a lantern. A creeping groundcover grows in a narrow planting bed at its feet.

right · This stone wall settles effortlessly into the landscape and blends in with the gray-painted house as well. It defines the patio without blocking views and provides extra seating during large gatherings.

RETAINING WALLS

Retaining walls are common elements of patios built on both gently and steeply sloping sites. They serve functional and aesthetic roles—holding back soil while adding color, texture, and dimension to a site. The ground above or behind a retaining wall can be transformed into a distinctive planting bed in which foliage and flowers are brought closer to eye level. The wall can also serve as a backdrop to plantings, or, with the inclusion of planting pockets, be a home to herbs, succulents, and other plants that prefer dry feet. If built at a height of 18 in. to 22 in., a retaining wall can provide a place to sit. (For children's areas, consider seat walls that are 12 in. to 15 in. high.) Steps often accompany retaining walls, and where they do, there is an opportunity to integrate interesting visual details such as contrasting materials, lighting fixtures, boulders, and planting pockets.

In addition to holding back soil, retaining walls also restrict the flow of water. For this reason, a drainage system should be part of the design. Local building codes should also be consulted, as they may call for building permits, inspections, or a soil analysis. On steep sites where the soil is unstable, walls may need to be reinforced with rebar and an engineer may need to be consulted.

As with freestanding walls, retaining walls may be constructed from stone that is dry laid or mortared, as well as brick and other masonry materials. Interlocking, modular concrete blocks have become an especially popular option for retaining walls, as they are affordable, easy to install, and come in a range of exterior finishes. All retaining walls need solid, below-grade foundations for support.

Freestanding walls built at different heights and finished with different colors or materials enclose this contemporary courtyard with character. A wooden bench is built into the lower stone wall, which runs perpendicular to a glass-tile-covered water feature. A planter built into the wall also adds visual interest.

Walls

CONCRETE AND STUCCO
$

- Poured concrete; concrete block; cinder block with stucco finish; or stacked, recycled concrete
- Poured concrete can be stained and texturized
- Stucco suitable for a variety of settings
- Poured concrete ideal for contemporary setting

BRICK
$$

- Uniform and easy to work with
- Subtle variations in color and texture
- Mortared construction
- Can be laid in open-weave pattern for air flow
- Can be laid with inset or protruding patterns for dimension

STONE
$$–$$$

- Fieldstone, stacked stone, or facing stone
- Dry laid or mortared, depending on height and use
- Natural look suitable to most landscapes

facing page • This patio features a series of curving stucco walls at different heights, finished in different colors. Low walls built from moss stone and capped with sandstone add contrasting colors and textures.

left • Poured concrete and concrete block walls can be covered in a stone veneer. This one was carefully crafted by a master stonemason to create what is referred to as an Anazasi-style stacked-stone pattern in which the stones are flat and stacked but vary in width.

below • A 4-ft. mortared brick wall surrounds planting beds in a courtyard. It is supported by a series of stone piers and topped with a running layer of capstones. The wall also serves as a visual backdrop for trees and vines.

Seat Walls

Seat walls help define a space without blocking views. Built at 14 in. to 16 in. high, they are the ideal height for sitting. For this reason, it is a good idea to finish them off with a capstone—a smooth-surfaced, cut stone that is 1½ in. to 2 in. thick and at least 12 in. wide—that won't snag clothing.

1. This seat wall has a slightly sloping back that doubles as the retaining wall for a hillside garden. Stone seats can be cold and hard, but cushions help soften and warm the bench both physically and visibly. 2. The terraced approach to this 4-ft. retaining wall both increases its stability and creates a seating area. The designer used local flagstone for the project. It overlooks a pool and woodland garden. 3. Large fieldstones were used to construct this seat wall (foreground). The thick, chiseled-edge bluestone cap provides a smooth and elegant finish. The stones in both the wall and paving range in tone from soft gray to light brown. 4. Slabs of stained concrete serve as a smooth seating surface for this seat wall, which was designed as part of a block retaining wall in a sunken patio. The clean lines of the hardscaping, along with the choice in furnishings, help create a contemporary look in this landscape.

A Relaxing Courtyard Patio

Despite its modest size, this side yard has plenty of sunny and shady places to retreat to (see the drawing)—three covered portals and several open patios—making it ideal for entertaining. Each varies in size, with some suitable for family or friends and others designed for more solitary enjoyment. The newest additions (shown in the photos) are patios located along the exterior walls and fences. The largest, which hosts a round dining table and umbrella, is laid in mortared flagstone. Another smaller patio, suitable for a single lounge chair, features dry-laid flagstone. And a third, even more casual but with a bit more space, is covered in gravel.

When Clemens & Associates was called in to create these spaces, the covered portals that were part of the home's architecture already existed. The homeowners wanted additional space for entertaining, some lawn, and a stream-like water feature. The yard was narrow, flanked by an existing southwestern-style stucco wall and coyote fencing, which is a vernacular fence style made from upright sticks. The land was also flat, without any distinguishing characteristics.

The concept for pulling this space together and giving it character was building a wall to create a raised bed against the fence. The wall, which is constructed from red- and buff-colored moss stone, adds warmth, texture, and dimension to the landscape while creating a planting bed, connecting the patio spaces, and

creating a logical place for the recirculating streambed. The low, stacked-stone wall and boulders also provide additional seating, which is especially nice when entertaining. It has a gentle curve that is repeated by the patios, creating a sense of unity and natural flow to the garden.

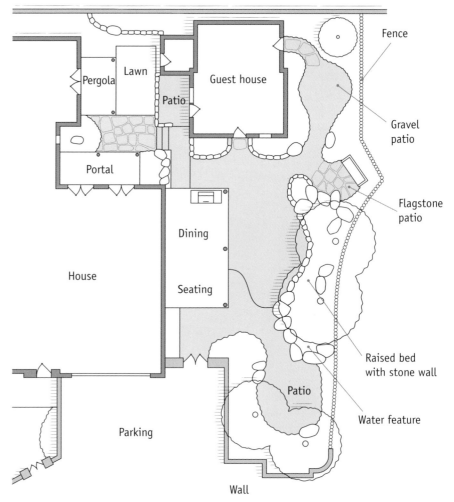

above • These two smaller spaces—one paved in stone, the other covered in gravel—are frequently used as patios for one or two people. Other times, they are used more for strolling or tending the garden. The boulder provides a place to rest briefly.

above • The retaining wall adds dimension to an otherwise flat site and creates a striking contrast to the vertical coyote fencing. Boulders anchor the wall and accent the beds. Both the wall stones and boulders are moss stone, which has a rich, earthy patina.

left • The new patio is enclosed by a southwestern-style stucco wall, wooden coyote fencing, garden beds, and a stone retaining wall. A recirculating garden stream originates at the patio end of the wall, gently splashing over various-sized river cobbles.

FENCES AND SCREENING

Fences come in ready-made segments, can be built from a wide range of precut or manufactured materials, or custom designed from unique construction materials. Their boards, slats, or pickets may be either tightly or widely spaced—dictating both the degree of privacy and amount of airflow within a patio. Among their chief advantages over masonry walls are affordability, ease of construction, and a smaller footprint.

Wooden fences are the most common. They have a rich design history, as their materials have been readily available to homeowners since the earliest days of our country's founding. Painted pickets are especially popular for their good looks, although split-rail, running-rail, wattle, and bamboo fences can be equally attractive in the right environments. Tall, board fencing provides a greater sense of privacy and can serve as a solid windbreak. Painted fences need a fresh coat of paint every three to five years; other wooden fences can be left to weather naturally. All are susceptible to warping, rot, and termite infestations, but a well-built and maintained fence should last for many years.

Lower-maintenance and longer-lasting alternatives to wood include a range of metals—wrought-iron, copper, aluminum, and steel are common. Yachting cable can be strung between wooden or metal posts for a contemporary look. Sheets of construction iron can be cut and welded into solid, one-of-a-kind fences. All fences, regardless of style, can be dressed up with interesting posts, gates, arches, and transitional arbors.

Hedges and other plantings can also be used to define boundaries, create privacy, and buffer the elements. They take time to grow, but are affordable and provide a strong connection to the landscape beyond. Planted closely together in staggered rows, evergreen shrubs will create a dense, almost impenetrable hedge. Mixed plantings, with shrub types planted in clusters, grow into an attractive tapestry for a garden wall.

above · This low Victorian fence was chosen more for decoration than screening, yet it clearly defines the patio boundary and adds character to the space. Lush perennials help provide a little privacy.

left · In lieu of hedges both fences and lattice can be covered with dense, evergreen vines. Ivy does the trick here and looks great with this dark green, decorative gate. The formal design and traditional plant choices give this courtyard a classic look.

right · The careful detailing in this fence kicks it up several notches from run-of-the-mill board fencing. The stain color matches the brick, chair, and large container to help create a clean, coordinated look.

Screening

Screening varies widely in cost, short-term impact, long-term durability, upkeep, and space requirements. It also varies in terms of visual and physical impact—with some options providing a dense barrier and others little more than a hint at screening. Here's a quick comparison of the cost and benefits of each.

MASONRY WALL
$$–$$$

- Classic appeal, ages well
- Sturdy, durable, low maintenance
- Stone, brick, block, stucco
- Height varies; can double as seating
- Freestanding or retaining walls
- Labor-intensive installation

PICKET FENCE
$$

- Classic charm; friendly rather than private
- Natural wood, painted wood, or wood composite
- Requires maintenance; moderate durability
- Moderately easy installation
- Narrow width, low height
- Great support for vines

PRIVACY FENCE
$

- Natural or stained wood boards
- Narrow width, tall height
- Easy to install, immediate impact

METAL FENCE
$$–$$$

- Prefabricated segments or custom built
- Aluminum, copper, steel, iron, cable
- Wide range of styles and finishes
- Narrow width, varied height
- Moderately easy installation

TRELLIS
$–$$

- Prefabricated sections or custom built
- Wood, metal, wire, or cable
- Easiest to install
- Open weave provides air flow
- Great support for vines
- Some immediate impact; needs time for vines to grow

EVERGREEN HEDGE
$

- Eco-friendly, living wall
- Seasonal interest (foliage, flowers, berries)
- Dense but not impenetrable
- Easy to install
- Needs time to grow

above • Virginia creeper scrambles over metal screening in this Santa Fe landscape, turning scarlet in fall. Boston ivy creates a similar effect in damper climates where Virginia creeper might get out of hand. The metal screening is attractive and effective with or without the vine.

above • An espaliered fruit tree adds a strong visual accent to this masonry wall. It has the added benefit of providing fruit in a minimum of physical space—an excellent option for small patios with limited space for trees or other plants.

above · Picket fences like this one are a friendly form of screening. They are lower than board fences, and their pickets can be spaced at varying widths. Here, the homeowners have created a sense of privacy without closing things off completely.

left · Solid fences provide privacy and good looks without breaking the bank. The cap that runs across the top of this board fence adds a nice finishing touch and increases its lifespan by reducing water absorption.

Shade Structures

Overhead structures come in a range of forms—from vine-covered arbors extending from a house wall, to fabric canopies strung between trees, to freestanding gazebos and pavilions in the landscape. What they have in common is shelter from the sun, and oftentimes from rain as well. Such overhead structures also help create a sense of intimacy, helping to define the boundaries of an outdoor room—even when the sides are open to views. They can be used to create a cozy backyard retreat to serve a multitude of purposes—cooking, dining, entertaining, curling up with a good book, or even providing a writer's or artist's retreat.

When designing a shade structure, keep in mind that bigger is usually better because the open landscape can easily dwarf outdoor structures. Consider scaling posts and beams up a size or two to give them some visual heft. Heftier materials also tend to warp less and last longer than their lighter-weight cousins. Choose rot-resistant materials, such as posts made from redwood, pressure-treated lumber, wood composites, metals, or poured concrete. Build them with strong, rust-resistant bolts rather than nails or standard screws, and sink them into concrete footings rather than directly into soil. Coated-metal roofing is long-lasting and looks great on garden structures.

Large structures with posts—such as arbors and pergolas—make good supports for outdoor lights and ceiling fans. They can also be beautiful when draped with substantial flowering vines such as Carolina jessamine (*Gelsemium sempervirens*), Lady Banks rose (*Rosa banksiae*), American wisteria (*Wisteria frutescens* 'Amethyst Falls'), trumpet honeysuckle (*Lonicera sempervirens*), and sweet autumn clematis (*Clematis terniflora*). Fruiting vines such as grapes are also favorites, although their fruit should be picked as it ripens to minimize any mess and to avoid attracting pests.

right • Eye-catching structures like this wooden pergola are suitable even for small yards. Setting the posts atop stone piers adds a decorative accent and helps deter termites, which have voracious wood-eating habits.

facing page left • This generous arbor extends from the back of the house out over the brick patio. Its brick color and slatted design make it unique. Structures such as this one provide a place to hang lights, lanterns, and ceiling fans.

top • This gazebo is a focal point and favorite destination in the landscape, both because it is painted white and because it is a formal element in a wooded garden. Although it is part of a naturalistic landscape, it sits on axis with the house at the other end of the garden.

above • Both the patio and roof were additions to this southwestern home. The roof is more about providing shade than rain protection, although it does both very effectively. The detailing in the posts matches the trim around the doors and windows of the home.

Shade Structures

Shade structures provide much-needed respite from the heat and screen views from neighbors' upstairs windows. Many also offer shelter from an unexpected shower. Even without these practical benefits, shade structures can add a strong, three-dimensional visual element to the landscape—whether freestanding or attached to a home.

MARKET UMBRELLA
$

- Portable—freestanding or for table
- Offers shade and some rain protection
- Many fabric colors and patterns
- Open and close as needed

AWNING
$$

- Attaches to home
- Offers protection from sun and light rain
- May be retractable
- Numerous fabric colors and patterns

SAIL CLOTH
$$

- Offers shade only
- Many colors, shapes, and sizes
- Stylish, contemporary option
- Can be custom designed

PERGOLA OR ARBOR
$$–$$$

- Arbors attach to house and can shade interior rooms
- Pergolas are freestanding structures
- Offer shade only
- Can be covered with fragrant or fruiting vines
- Require maintenance

PAVILION OR GAZEBO
$$–$$$

- Offers shade and shelter from rain
- Permanent structures that require maintenance
- Usually require a poured foundation
- Can reflect architectural style of home

PORTICO OR PORCH
$$$

- Offers shade and shelter from rain
- Permanent structures that are part of house
- May require a permit to build
- Can often be screened for bug protection

above • Awnings come in a range of colors. They are an attractive and affordable option for providing shade over a small space just outside of a home. This one is black to match the home's trim, doors, and patio furniture.

above · An old-fashioned, cushioned porch swing hangs from this attached arbor, which both creates a shady garden spot and helps shade the adjacent room of the house. The white house, arbor, swing, containers, and flowers all work together to create a bright, lovely setting.

right · Striped shade cloth suits this colorful garden just right—accenting and coordinating without overpowering. It offers a cool respite in a hot landscape and helps establish a magical atmosphere.

left · This poolside pavilion features an outdoor kitchen (background) and fireplace, a comfortable seating area, and a ceiling fan. The fireplace was built from local limestone and makes it possible to retreat outdoors even on mild winter days in the Hill Country of southern Texas.

A Poolside Pavilion for Cooking and Dining

Although Joy LeBlanc is an interior decorator, she doesn't limit herself to interiors. She has discovered that outdoor spaces can be just as inviting and has adapted many of her design strategies in this poolside pavilion.

Architecturally, the structure ties in with the design of the home. Matching columns, paint colors, and roof shingles help create a sense of continuity. The roofline, however, is unique, with both covered-roof and arbor sections, providing some protection from the elements while retaining a bright, open atmosphere. Because the late-afternoon sun can be brutal in summer, curtains were hung on the western side of the pavilion. They were made from the same material used on poolside lounge chairs, which helps tie the pool deck and pavilion together visually.

Inside the pavilion, which is used daily by family members, including teenaged children who enjoy hanging out by the pool with friends, is an outdoor kitchen that offers a variety of ways to cook. A gas grill is the workhorse, where most meals are prepared. But there is also a side burner, which is helpful when warming soups or side dishes; a gas-fueled pizza oven, which the children especially enjoy; and a smoker for cooking meats slowly. There is also an undercounter refrigerator for drinks and condiments, as well as for keeping meats cool until they are ready to be tossed on the grill. Countertops are covered in granite. The outdoor kitchen cabinets double as low walls for the pavilion—helping to create a sense of privacy and buffering winds that blow across the adjacent golf course.

above • The outdoor kitchen is laid out in an L-shape that doubles as a pavilion wall. It features a pizza oven, undercounter refrigerator, gas grill, side burner, and smoker. Both short and long sections of counter space are included for food prep and serving.

above · This pavilion is a partially roofed structure—providing protection for both the cooking and dining areas, but with the atmosphere of an arbor or pergola. The flooring is raised slightly, both to call attention to the space and to divert runoff in a heavy rain since this was built on a sloping site.

left · Curtains in the pavilion, which screen those enjoying dinner or drinks from the late-afternoon sun, are coordinated with the cushions on poolside lounge chairs, creating a sense of unity throughout the outdoor living area.

Shade Arbors and Pergolas

Arbors and pergolas offer a shady respite in a sunny landscape. These open-beamed structures can be freestanding or attached to a home and often serve as a focal point in the landscape. Although their defining lines are often blurred, arbors are generally attached to a house and pergolas are freestanding. Both make excellent supports for vigorous vines.

1. This arbor combines formal, painted, architectural posts and lower-maintenance, unfinished beams. The posts blend in with the formal garden, but the beams don't have to be painted (which can be a challenge when they're covered with vines). 2. Oversized posts and beams best suit the scale of a broad landscape and also do a good job supporting large, fast-growing vines such as wisteria. The raised, stone flooring defines this pavilion as a destination and not just a pass-through space. 3. This free-standing pergola design works well in the narrow space of a small backyard. The curved outer edge provides an elegant touch and echoes the shape of the paved patio surface below.

3

PATHS AND

Paths show you where to go and help you get there safely. They also set the tone for the journey—whether quick and businesslike or a more relaxed and enjoyable experience.

STEPS

Pathways

Paths serve both functional and aesthetic roles in the landscape. At their most basic level, they lead you from one place to another—both physically and visually. Your eye naturally follows a path—whether it clearly leads to the front door or piques your curiosity by disappearing along a curve to an unknown destination. Your feet follow paths, too. They indicate the way a homeowner expects for you to traverse the property—to reach the main entry, the back door, the pool, the garden, or other destinations in the landscape. But paths can also set the tone for a journey—signaling areas you can move through quickly or should slow down to experience more intimately.

Paths should be designed based on their intended use—firm underfoot and wide enough for people to pass comfortably. They should be designed in a style and with materials that complement the home's architecture or settle comfortably into landscape. These materials run the gamut from flagstone, brick, concrete, concrete pavers, and tile to gravel, crushed stone, and

mulch. Depending upon their purpose and location, paths may be mortared or dry laid. How a path is designed also determines what kind of experience one has along the way. They may be short or long, narrow or wide, and straight or winding. Wide, straight, and smooth paths generally mean business; they get you to your destination in the shortest time possible. Narrow, winding paths extend an invitation to slow down and enjoy the landscape around you.

There are three common categories of paths. Primary paths are the most important in the landscape. They tend to lead to the house, are used daily, and are the most formal. Secondary paths are more casual but still highly functional, connecting key areas in the landscape. Tertiary paths may be more about experiencing the garden, reaching a getaway location, or accessing utilitarian parts of the landscape. They are often reserved more for the use of the homeowners rather than guests.

right • Pathways don't have to be uniform. This one is laid in an unexpected, irregular fashion. It catches your attention and slows you down, but doesn't impede you from reaching your destination.

far right • This straight, broad path leaves no doubts about where it leads—directly to the main entry of this home. Passage can be fast and efficient but is also elegant and inviting. The materials and the way in which they've been used signal a sense of formality.

facing page • While front paths are more often mortared than other kinds of paths, they can also be dry laid. This broad, rectangular cut-stone path clearly leads to an entry and suits the contemporary style and clean lines of the home.

PRIMARY PATHS

Primary paths are those that get the most use and typically lead to the house. Paths leading to the front door from the street or driveway are good examples, although they may also lead to a side door or beneath a breezeway connecting a home and garage. These are the paths used by guests, delivery persons, and homeowners on a daily basis.

Since most primary paths lead to the house, they should tie in visually with the architecture of the home. Select materials that echo those in the home's construction, reflect its architectural style, or complement its colors and materials. These paths should be easily traversed and wide enough for two people to walk comfortably, side by side—42 in. to 48 in. is a good guide. They should also be in scale with the house. A large, two-story house on a broad suburban lawn demands a wider path than a small cottage on a compact urban lot.

The best options for primary paths include stone, brick, tile, concrete, and concrete pavers. Most are mortared or very tightly laid for durability due to their heavy use. This also helps prevent loose materials from being tracked into the house and eases snow removal in winter. They may be winding, straight, or make one or more angled jogs. They may also integrate steps and landings. Plantings along either side or at grade changes can enhance, but should not impede, passage. Widening a primary path at one or both ends is an effective way to call attention to its beginning and destination. Pillars, posts, boulders, lampposts, arbors, and planting beds can also help highlight a passageway, while a circular motif or unique paving pattern near the front door can add a special decorative accent. Constructing the walkway along a natural course between two points is a good way to keep others on course. A raised edge or adjacent planting bed can also serve this purpose well.

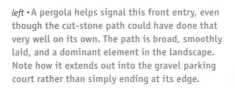

left • A pergola helps signal this front entry, even though the cut-stone path could have done that very well on its own. The path is broad, smoothly laid, and a dominant element in the landscape. Note how it extends out into the gravel parking court rather than simply ending at its edge.

right • Rather than place all of the steps at one point, this site was graded so that the steps could be broken up and spaced between stretches of gently curving path. This makes the approach more enjoyable and encourages one to enjoy the garden.

left • The simple lines of this farmhouse call for an equally simple approach to the home. A straight, wide, cut-stone path that enters from the drive (rather than from the street) does the trick. The steps are also simply designed with matching cut-stone risers and stone slab treads.

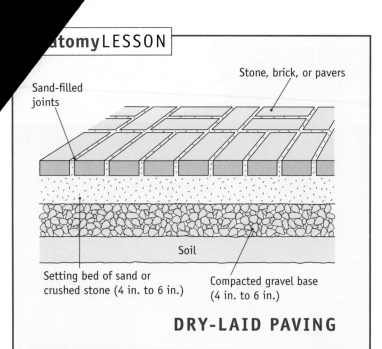

Sand-filled joints

Stone, brick, or pavers

Soil

Setting bed of sand or crushed stone (4 in. to 6 in.)

Compacted gravel base (4 in. to 6 in.)

DRY-LAID PAVING

above · Rustic homes benefit from a more casual treatment of pathways. This dry-laid path of irregular flagstone is still wide enough for two to walk side by side, but much less formal than a straight, mortared path.

right · This side entry is still considered a primary path because it is the most frequently used in the landscape. Positioned between the garage and house, it is used daily by the homeowners and close friends. The path is smooth and wide and provides easy access to the breezeway.

above · Slight grade changes can be addressed by sloping the path, creating a small ramp as shown here, or some combination of the two. It is a good alternative for those who may have difficulty traversing steps.

SECONDARY PATHS

Whether they extend from primary paths or stand on their own, secondary paths are perhaps the most diverse walkways. They may lead from the patio to the swimming pool, provide access between the front yard and backyard, wind through a garden, or connect the back door and garage.

Often utilitarian in nature, secondary paths may be wide enough to accommodate carts and wheelbarrows—2 ft. to 3 ft. is common. This can be helpful whether hauling mulch to the garden or a cooler filled with drinks to the pool. Other paths are more pedestrian-oriented in nature—providing access to a patio or play space, winding their way through a garden, or leading to a destination patio at the edge of the woods. Such paths can be made from any materials and should be chosen based on their function and whether the paths relate more to the house or landscape, along with cost, availability, and ease of installation.

If secondary paths get just as much use in winter as in summer, a smooth or mortared surface will make it easier to shovel snow in cold climates. If the path winds through a garden and the intent is to slow a traveler down, consider allowing creeping plants such as woolly thyme (*Thymus pseudonlanuginosus*), blue star creeper (*Laurentia fluviatilis*), or mazus (*Mazus repens*) to fill in between dry-laid stones, bricks, or pavers.

top · This secondary path, which leads through a side-yard garden, is formal in style yet narrow in width. The brick is mortared, but laid just wide enough for one person or a wheelbarrow to pass.

right · Although not as wide as a front path, the widely spaced, square pavers are just formal enough to complement this traditional home and the boxwood parterre. They are a perfect choice for a frequently used secondary pathway.

above • Even among secondary paths, widths can vary widely. The steppingstone path leading from the house to the patio uses large stones and is two stones wide, while the one leading through the garden and around the side of the house uses small stones and is just one stone wide.

left • This path is wide enough for carrying things to a destination patio and for tending the garden. The pavers are made from concrete embedded with pebbles. They are durable and blend in with the surrounding landscape materials.

Paths for Lingering

When the removal of a large Monterey pine created an open, sunny space in a previously shady garden, landscape architect Richard McPherson was called in to redesign the narrow rear and side gardens surrounding this home. The client, Joan, wanted to create a pleasing view from the living room, a space that could be used for entertaining, and a place with a sense of serenity.

The focal point of the new garden is an elegant, curving stone seat wall that is viewed from inside the house. It forms the edge of a small patio, providing an open space for entertaining or pulling up a few chairs on a sunny afternoon, or just pausing to rest on the wall. An urn fountain sits nearby, masking neighborhood noise and adding the peaceful gurgle of water to the setting. Joan loves roses, and so the fragrant 'Honey Perfume' was planted behind the seat wall.

To connect the house to the garden, two small deck and step areas were created. The decks, along with the patio and other areas of the garden, are connected by a series of paths that wend around the house and through the garden. Mortared flagstone with light brown grout joints form the paths that widen to create the patio. In other places, flagstone steppingstones and mulch paths are used.

Because the property is small and located close to neighbors and the street, clumping bamboo was planted as a dense, living fence. Other key plants include ornamental grasses, creeping thyme, roses, ferns, and a small Japanese maple. Joan has also placed several pieces of sculpture and whimsical art throughout the garden to give it added personality.

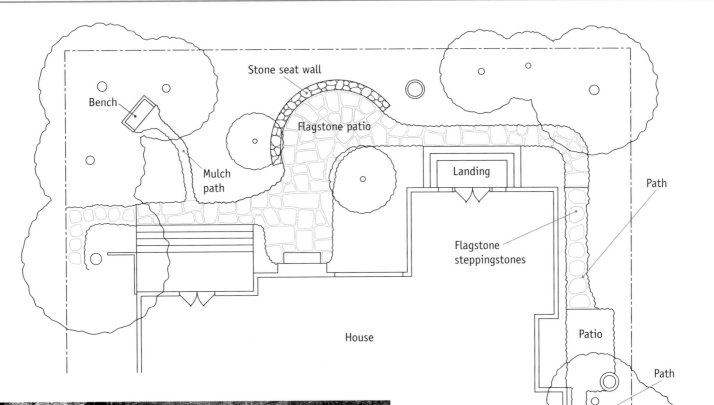

Bench

Stone seat wall

Mulch
path

Flagstone patio

Landing

Flagstone
steppingstones

Path

House

Patio

Path

top • The Cameron Dark flagstone is mortared but left
irregular along the path's edges for added visual
interest. This path connects the patio with one
of the small decks and leads through the shady
garden area.

far left • A large urn was transformed into a bubbling
fountain to help create a soothing setting and to
help mask noise from the nearby street. The urn's
colors were carefully chosen to blend quietly into
the garden and to coordinate with the stone.

left • The stone seat wall, which anchors the patio
and can be viewed from the living room window,
features a veneer of Harlan Valley stone. The
homeowner enjoys the openness of the space and
likes sitting on the wall. When entertaining, she
sometimes brings out a few chairs for guests.

TERTIARY PATHS

The least formal, narrowest, and most intriguing paths are the tertiary paths, sometimes referred to as garden paths. They are commonly only 12 in. to 16 in. wide—just wide enough for one person to walk along. They are the most likely to be dry laid or made from loose materials such as gravel, crushed stone, or mulch. Steppingstones of all shapes, sizes, and materials—from natural stone and recycled bricks to handmade, decorated, poured-concrete steppingstones—are also popular for tertiary paths, although just about any materials can be used.

Tertiary paths may lead through a garden, into the woods, around the corner of the house, or to utilitarian areas such as the garden shed, compost heap, trash bins, or water spigots. Often, they are intended strictly for homeowner use and may only be used in warmer months. Although they may be slightly uneven underfoot, steppingstones should still be safely secured by placing them in the soil, flush with ground level, rather than simply laid on top of the ground.

top · Gravel is an excellent choice for secondary paths, providing a pleasant crunch underfoot when walked on. It needs to be weeded regularly and replenished occasionally, but it is easy to spread and maintain.

above · Steppingstones can vary in size throughout a path. They can also be laid in irregular patterns or, as demonstrated here, side by side. Just about any kind of stone works as long as it has a flat surface and is thick enough to withstand the weight of traffic.

right · While primary paths usually make their destination clear, secondary paths are often much more intriguing. This one curves and disappears around a bend, generating a sense of curiosity and inviting you into the garden to explore.

Mulch—A Sustainable Pathway Alternative

When it comes to casual, tertiary pathways through the garden and landscape, mulch is an affordable and sustainable alternative to brick, stone, concrete, and tile. A recycled material—made by grinding or shredding the bark of trees harvested for other purposes—mulch is an organic material that nourishes the soil as it breaks down and is a permeable surface that encourages rainwater to soak into the soil rather than to run off into a drainage ditch. The only downside to mulch is that it must be replenished often—annually in most climates.

Steppingstone Paths

Steppingstone paths are typically set in the earth and more widely spaced than formal dry-laid paths. Rather than casually walking along the path, you must more consciously "step" from one paver to another, which calls for a slower pace. Pavers may be laid one after another in a single row or in a more random or irregular fashion. And while most are made of stone, pavers in other materials can be easily adapted.

1. These stone slabs, laid parallel but with varying lengths, not only provide access to points in the landscape but also create an eye-catching pattern that is visually compelling. Tufts of blue fescue have been planted in the spaces between and will create a contrasting texture against the smooth stones. **2.** Rather than laying these round, concrete steppingstones in grass, the designer placed them amid an edged river cobble path. The flat stones are easier to walk on than the cobbles, and the contrasting sizes, shapes, and textures dress up the pathway. **3.** These steppingstones were placed in the lawn beside the mixed shrub border. It is a subtle, yet striking touch that is much appreciated in landscapes when the lawn is still damp from morning dew or after a rainfall. **4.** Cut pieces of irregular flagstone were assembled and mortared in frames and then used as formal steppingstones between a patio and pool deck. They match the pool decking but signal a transition in the landscape.

1

Creative Paving

Mixing and matching materials is an easy way to liven up paving, whether on pathways or patios. Materials of contrasting color, shape, size, and texture can be used to create patterns and mosaics, add decorative accents to paving joints and borders, or even create an eye-catching focal point in the landscape. Even materials not typically used for paving—such as recycled glass beads, bits of broken pottery, or shells—can be mixed in for accent.

1. Inspired by *Alice in Wonderland*, this brick pathway almost appears to tumble down the hill. The zigzagging manner in which it is designed, as well as the cut, angular bricks laid in a crazy paving fashion contribute to this impression. **2.** The dwarf sweet flag that fills in between these pavers creates a dramatic visual texture that is accentuated by the tall spires of horsetails. Both plants like damp soil. Dwarf black mondo would provide an equally dramatic effect under drier conditions. **3.** These granite pavers were laid out in a flowing pattern to create an intriguing passageway. Complex designs such as this one are laid out on paper first and then cut to specification by a skilled stonemason. **4.** Several design strategies work together to make this an eye-catching entry. Both the color and texture of the stones and border provide a striking contrast, and the unexpected, asymmetric way in which the path meets the steps calls attention to the transition.

Steps and Stairs

Transitions between grades are among the more challenging landscape features to design. But when designed well, they not only make it safe and easy to negotiate a slope, but they also can serve as attractive focal points in the landscape. They can also help set the tone for the space one is entering—whether it is the house, a patio, or other location in the landscape.

Safety, of course, is a critical element of step and stair design. The rise and run of steps should be both comfortable and natural, which tend to fall within a limited range. Materials that get slippery when wet should be avoided. Local codes or common sense may call for railings, which are always a good idea when there are three or more steps. Calling attention to the grade change will help eliminate surprises and potential accidents. This can be accomplished in any number of ways, including paving the edge of upper patios or paths in a different material or making the steps themselves a different color or material from path or patio paving. Special elements placed in the adjacent landscape—perhaps a post, boulder, or shrub—can help highlight steps. Landscape lighting—whether built into the steps or wall, positioned overhead, or placed on short posts adjacent to the steps—will ease passage at night.

Steps can be fashioned from many of the same materials as pathways and patios—stone, brick, and concrete pavers are excellent choices. Wooden stairs are also common, especially leading from the house or a deck. Broad steps feel at home in the landscape; make them at least as wide as the paths. And if you need a flight of steps to navigate a steep hillside, consider adding a landing every seven steps or so. Winding or zigzagging staircases are also more compelling and easier to negotiate than a flight of long, straight stairs.

top • Several strategies work together to make climbing this steep hillside a pleasurable experience: landings for rest, the zigzagging layout that breaks up the climb, and interesting plantings to enjoy along the way.

bottom • Corner steps are an interesting alternative to straight steps. These bluestone steps offer easy access in two directions, as well. Lighting and an iron handrail help make the steps safe for passage.

Granite and red brick are beautiful companions. Here they team up in a flight of garden steps with a small landing in the middle. The steps broaden as they near the lower patio.

FORMAL STEPS AND LANDINGS

The most formal steps and stairways in the landscape are those that lead to the front door. Since few homes are built at ground level, most have at least one step, often onto a landing. The minimum width for a landing is generally 3 ft. or the width of the door, but adding at least 1 ft. in both directions will greatly increase convenience; front landings are usually larger. Entries with screen doors that swing out rather than into the house also need a larger landing. Indeed, one of the easiest ways to make over a simple front entry is to expand the landing into a front patio with room for two or more chairs and a few container plantings. The existing concrete stoops that come with many older homes can also be spruced up by adding a layer of thin paving materials—called facing—such as bluestone or brick pavers (which are half the width of facing bricks).

When the entry is higher, consider broad steps that run 6 ft. or more wide. At a minimum, steps should be 3 ft. wide, and 5 ft. is needed for two people to walk side by side. Deeper treads (the part you step on) and shorter risers (the upright part) will encourage a slower pace. Outdoors, steps with a rise of 5½ in. to 7 in. and a tread of 12 in. to 18 in. are common. Steps can feature curved rather than straight treads and flair outward like open arms. Unique or artisan-crafted handrails can spruce up an entry staircase, and warm-toned paving materials can make an entry feel welcoming.

Formal steps are appropriate in many side and backyard settings as well, particularly accompanying more traditional homes. Classic materials like brick and cut stone laid in patterns quickly dress up a site. The materials used for formal steps and landings should take cues from the home—complementing its style, colors, materials, and architectural elements.

A curving stone wall complements a winding stone staircase that leads to this home's front entry. Instead of railings, the stone wall continues, staggered, up the steps. The bluestone caps on the walls are echoed in the stair treads.

above • Although they are irregularly shaped, the stones in these risers and the adjacent stone wall were carefully chosen and assembled. They are mortared for a secure fit, and the mortar has been partially scraped from the joints to give a dry-laid look. The stair treads are contrasting, light-colored, cut stones.

above • Shallow risers and deep treads encourage a relaxed pace as you move toward the entry of this home. Bricks with mortared joints along the pathway and step edges hold bricks laid side by side without mortared joints in place.

left • Taking cues from classic European design, these broad steps are large enough to be landings. Each tread is filled with lawn. Although the steps must be mowed, they nicely tie together the upper and lower lawns.

anatomyLESSON

STEPS

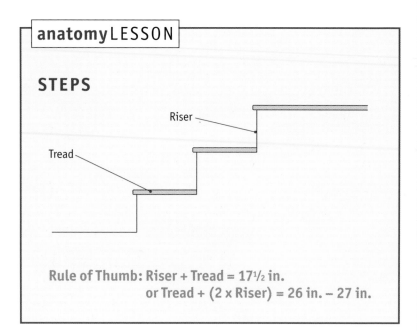

Riser

Tread

Rule of Thumb: Riser + Tread = 17½ in.
or Tread + (2 x Riser) = 26 in. – 27 in.

top • Pattern is important in contemporary designs, where materials are often neutral in tone. The pattern in the gate, fence, and plantings allows the smooth-surfaced steps to stand out boldly in the landscape. Frequent landings offer places to pause.

right • The bluestone treads on these steps are bull-nosed, or rounded. It is a treatment that dresses up stone in a formal setting. The broad landing gives you a chance to stop and smell the roses.

right • Picking up the pattern and materials of adjacent walls in the step risers is an effective way to create a sense of unity in a transitional area. The walls mark the transition, while the steps signal a grade change. The walls also provide support in lieu of a rail.

bottom right • It's impossible to miss these broad sweeping steps. Their width and styling show the way to the home's front entry. Broad treads and shallow risers encourage a casual pace for enjoying the garden.

INFORMAL STEPS

Along secondary and tertiary pathways, informal steps are more common. Mortared steps with smooth surfaces may be most appropriate for utilitarian paths or those that are used frequently. But once you move out into the landscape, it is common to design and build steps that are more rustic in nature and laid without mortar. Their surfaces may not be as smooth, although they should still provide safe passage.

Stone is the most common material used for informal steps, although materials such as railroad ties and recycled concrete are equally appropriate. It can also be fun to mix and match materials in a more eclectic setting. Filling steps edged in brick or railroad ties with pea gravel or crushed gravel is also an option. Consider growing small ferns or other tiny, creeping plants in the cracks and crevices—especially if the goal is to create a garden experience. Both the steps and the plants will give you and your guests reason to slow down and enjoy the landscape.

When undertaking a construction project, it is also helpful to plan ahead. Will someone in your family need a ramp rather than steps in the not-too-distant future? Even if you don't add them now, thinking about how they could be added easily later can save money in the long run.

right • Landscape or railroad timbers can often be salvaged and reused in residential landscaping. Here, they are back-filled with pebbles to create the treads of garden steps. Larger stones placed along the edge help keep the pebbles in place.

facing page top • On relatively level lots, one or two steps may be all that are needed. They are important not only for moving about, but also for adding dimension to an otherwise flat plot of land. The plants growing in the joints between the stones add textural interest to the smooth slabs.

facing page bottom • Large stones or small boulders with relatively flat surfaces make excellent steps in a garden setting. These may not measure up with a level, but they are perfect in a place where you enjoy the contemplation of each step.

Improving Handicap Access

Smooth paved surfaces, gently sloping paths, and handicap ramps make a landscape much more inviting and accessible to those with limited mobility. The Americans with Disabilities Act (ADA) has established national guidelines for ramps. State and local building codes may also apply, and homeowner associations may require certain cosmetic features. The ADA guidelines specify that a ramp should not exceed 1 in. per ft. of rise (1:12 ratio) or a total rise of 30 in., that a minimum 60-in.-square landing be included at both the top and bottom of the ramp, and that the ramp be at least 3 ft. wide. If the rise exceeds 6 in. or the length exceeds 6 ft., handrails must also be included on both sides. Ramps may be made from a variety of landscape materials, as long as they are sturdy, safe, and easy to negotiate, which makes it possible to design them to blend in with the architecture and landscape.

Rails don't have to look like those used on buildings or in public spaces—they just have to provide support. This hand-forged rail snakes down a hillside where railroad ties and mortared bricks have been paired for casual steps.

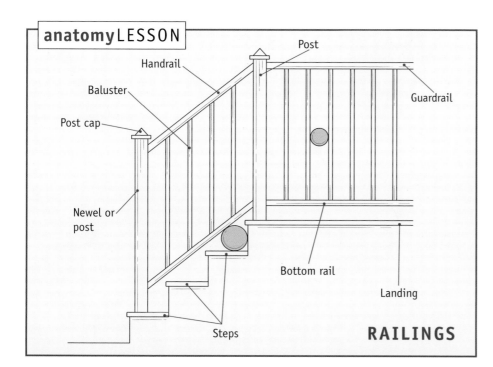

anatomyLESSON

Post

Handrail

Baluster

Guardrail

Post cap

Newel or
post

Bottom rail

Landing

Steps

RAILINGS

above • Wooden steps can be used throughout the landscape as well as leading to the house or deck. This flight connects a pool deck and pool house. The cables on the railing also are used on an upper deck above the pool.

left • When stepped upon, the herbs growing in the cracks of these steps will release their sweet fragrance. A variety of thymes have been tucked in here and there for visual and sensory appeal.

Steps

Unlike paths, which are essentially
two-dimensional, steps have
unique three-dimensional qualities
worth exploring and exploiting.
They run the gamut in terms of
design styles and materials, and
offer a perfect spot for mixing and
matching materials. Steps can also
be creatively woven into a sloping
hillside with plantings and boulders.

1. The steps leading from this deck are made more manageable by adding a landing and more interesting by having a divided lower flight leading in opposite directions. The solid rail, inset tree design, bench, and contrasting panels dress up the steps. 2. Three different stones—moss stone, Arizona sandstone, and black river pebbles—have been combined for an eye-catching effect in these steps. The change in direction, along with the walls, also adds visual interest. 3. Decorative, patterned tiles are often used to face the risers on steps, adding a colorful accent to the landscape. This is especially common with Mediterranean-style architecture. 4. Circular steps take up more space than straight steps but can serve as a dramatic focal point in a landscape or garden. These circular steps are also punctuated by low pillars topped with elegant lanterns that light the way onto the upper lawn.

TRANSITIONAL GATES, POSTS, AND ARBORS

One of the best ways to signal an entry and mark a significant transition in a landscape is by installing gates, posts, arbors, or arches. Such architectural elements should reflect the architectural style of the home—whether traditional, contemporary, or rustic. They can be painted white to catch the eye or left natural so as not to draw attention away from the house. And while they may, in themselves, be focal points, their real role is to call attention to a change in place, pace, or experience.

Transitional elements mark passageways to different parts of the landscape—from the driveway to the front path, from the garden to the patio, from the front yard to the side yard. They are like doorways inside a home, marking different experiences— from a utilitarian area to a passageway or from a recreational or gardening area to one designed for cooking and dining. They cause us to stop, pause, and take note of our surroundings.

left · This pair of highly detailed wrought-iron gates allows a glimpse through a small courtyard and into the backyard beyond, creating a sense of intrigue. The gates also serve as decorative elements in the garden.

below · An open gate is a sign of welcome. The low height, widely spaced pickets, and rustic styling also signal that these homeowners enjoy visiting with passersby. While the fence is used more for character and definition, it could easily contain a small dog when the gate is closed.

far left · A granite pier with a thick, bluestone cap marks the transition from this parking court to the front path. Narrow stones, as well as a few upright stones, vary the pattern in the stonework.

left · This classically designed, arched arbor clearly signals a transition into a new garden space—a patio with a boxwood parterre. The lattice along its sides and rungs across the top are the perfect support for vines.

Gates

Gates can signal an entry, provide security, screen views, contain pets in an enclosed space, and dress up a wall or fence. Depending upon their height and density, they can either be a sign of welcome or an indication that you prefer your privacy. They also can be simply designed or stand out as highly decorative elements in the landscape.

1. This rustic gate, which has been framed like a window, suits the regional southwestern architecture and offers a focal point in the garden. Because the gap at the bottom is just enough to allow the gate to swing freely, it could keep a small dog secured in the courtyard. 2. The contemporary gate leading from this narrow side yard was custom-designed for the homeowner. Instead of upright pickets, it features horizontal boards spaced closely to help maintain a sense of privacy. 3. This classic picket-fence gate features traditional iron hardware. It has been hung on sturdy posts topped with decorative finials. The pickets match the styling, height, and spacing of the pickets in the fence. 4. A custom fence was designed to complement the Craftsman styling in the home. Leaving a modest gap beneath the gate improves airflow in the narrow side-yard passageway without sacrificing the screening.

Transitional Arbors

Arbors are an enchanting way to highlight a passage. They help create a sense of drama when passing from one space into a uniquely different one. With their height, they stand out as focal points in the landscape, and their design can help define the style of the garden. Arbors can stand alone or be accompanied by gates, and they are the perfect support for climbing roses and other flowering vines.

3

4

1. This eye-catching arbor is reminiscent of an acorn, spade, or heart. It is both broad and tall and features a unique gate, as well. Vigorous vines are quickly wending their way up the rungs toward the sky.

2. This Victorian-style arbor has a roof, gate, and detailed woodwork. It has also been wired for lighting, with a lantern hanging from its center truss. It makes an interesting and inviting alternative to a lamppost.

3. What makes this arbor unique is its width, allowing two people to pass beneath simultaneously. It is sturdily built and blends in with the naturalistic landscaping surrounding this home. **4.** A single, sturdy arch built from heavy beams spans this brick-and-paver pathway, which leads to an outdoor living area and pool in the backyard. Its size and uniqueness make a bold statement in the landscape.

OUTDOOR

With the introduction of so many outdoor kitchen amenities,

the entire cooking and dining experience can be moved outdoors,

COOKING

where we can gather with friends and family

in a relaxed atmosphere.

AND DINING

Outdoor Kitchens

Outdoor kitchens rank among the most popular additions to backyard patios. Indeed, they have become a focal point for outdoor living. While freestanding grills now come with a dazzling array of features, outdoor kitchens kick convenience up a notch by offering counter space for food preparation and serving, as well as a host of other amenities to enhance the outdoor cooking experience. Sinks help simplify cleanup, while under-counter refrigerators keep drinks and condiments cold. Cabinets store frequently used items where you need them; side burners make it a snap to prepare side dishes, and countertop extensions increase seating capacity. Many kitchens also include wood-burning ovens for baking pizzas and casseroles.

Whether prefabricated or custom-built, all cabinetry should be made to withstand the weather. Choose durable materials that won't crack, peel, rust, rot, or warp. All appliances should be rated for outdoor use. Adding extra GFCI (ground-fault circuit interrupter) electrical outlets will make it easy to plug in kitchen appliances, personal electronic devices, radios, and fans. Also, don't forget the lighting: Task lights will aid with food preparation and cooking, while ambient lighting can be used to create just the right mood for dining. Placing lights on separate switches and dimmers makes it easy to create the right atmosphere.

In some jurisdictions, outdoor kitchens are subject to building and fire-safety codes. Even when they're not, safety is always a consideration. Grills and wood-burning ovens can reach extremely hot temperatures and should be positioned away from high-traffic areas; a run of counters can serve as a protective barrier. Give grills a generous buffer from trees, roof overhangs, and items that could melt or catch fire. Beneath a roof or overhang, a hood vent may be necessary. And finally, place grills downwind of prevailing breezes and away from dining and entertaining areas to minimize smoke and fumes.

above · This basic but attractive grilling island features a gas grill, elegant wood cabinetry, and stone countertops. The wood holds up well in this dry Southwest climate beneath the shade of the portico.

facing page top left · Antique and recycled objects pack this outdoor kitchen with personality. With the wood-burning oven and generous kitchen table, it's the perfect place to host a pizza party. Lanterns help create a festive atmosphere after dark.

facing page top right · An L-shaped kitchen configuration makes good use of limited space. Here, the grill is on the far end, away from a seating area. The open counter is convenient for the chef and for serving. The brick and limestone are sturdy and blend in with the architecture.

facing page bottom · This grilling cabinet features a gas grill, side burner, and undercounter refrigerator, as well as ample storage and counter space. The stainless steel doors, appliances, and countertops offer contemporary styling and easy care. Task lights hang overhead.

Grills, Smokers, and Wood-burning Ovens

The range of grills and features can be overwhelming. Look for a sturdy unit that suits the size of the meals you plan to cook. Larger units simply waste fuel, and features you don't really need just run up the price tag. Easy-to-read controls, easily accessible ash and drip pans, cool-touch handles, and multiple vents for greater temperature control are all important features to look for.

PORTABLE GRILL
$

- Small and easy to move
- Perfect for picnics, tailgating, and small spaces
- Charcoal, gas, and electric models

FREESTANDING GRILL
$–$$

- Easy to move, often on wheels
- Flat-topped, dome, and barrel models
- Range of sizes and cooking surfaces
- May feature built-in accessories
- Charcoal, gas, pellet, and electric models

CERAMIC COOKER
$$-$$$

- Usually portable, on wheels
- Uses hardwood charcoal
- For grilling, smoking, and convection cooking
- Well insulated for moister foods

SMOKER
$–$$

- Easy to move
- Designed specifically for smoking
- May also be used for grilling
- Charcoal and pellet models

SMOKER-GRILL
$–$$

- Usually easy to move, may have wheels
- Typically two grilling surfaces
- Designed for both smoking and grilling
- Charcoal models

CABINET GRILL
$$–$$$

- Easy to move, usually on wheels
- Built-in storage and workspace
- May feature built-in accessories
- Charcoal and gas models common

SLIDE-IN GRILL
$$–$$$

- Permanent fixture, slides into a cabinet/island
- Island provides workspace
- Includes built-in storage beneath grill
- May feature built-in accessories
- Charcoal, gas, and pellet models common

DROP-IN GRILL
$$–$$$

- Permanent fixture, drops into cabinet/island
- Island provides workspace
- Does not include built-in storage
- May feature built-in grill accessories
- Charcoal, gas, and pellet models common

WOOD-BURNING OVEN
$$$

- Permanent construction
- Can be used for baking or grilling
- Takes time to build up temperature
- Can be used for slow-cooking many dishes
- Does not include accessories
- Custom storage cabinet may be built
- Uses wood for fuel

top • Drop-in grills come in a range of standard sizes that allow them to be matched with a wide range of custom or prefabricated cabinetry. This one has a sleek design and is set in custom wood cabinetry with concrete countertops.

right • This retro-style grilling cabinet looks more like a stove than a grill. It features a three-burner grill, granite countertops, and lots of cabinets and drawers for storage. The black cabinet and iron furniture are striking against the white limestone, recalling old-fashioned black-and-white kitchens.

top · This freestanding, cabinet-style grill features a large cooking surface, a warming shelf above the cooking area, enclosed storage space beneath, and short shelves on either side. It can be moved to another location, if needed.

above · This outdoor kitchen features both a stainless-steel, slide-in grilling cabinet and a custom-built, wood-burning oven. With a little practice, just about anything can be baked or grilled in the oven.

CONFIGURING THE OUTDOOR KITCHEN

Outdoor kitchens can be built against a wall, along the periphery of a patio, or as freestanding islands that offer accessibility on all sides on a patio. They can also be configured in a range of layouts to satisfy an outdoor chef's demands and to adapt to a range of spaces. The size of the grill, number of appliances, and need for counter space all play into the equation. Whether or not bar seating is desired is also a key factor. Seating can be provided by extending the overhang on the counter, adding a raised bar, or attaching an extension table.

Common cabinet layout options include a single-run counter; double-run or galley counters; and L-shaped, U-shaped, and G-shaped counter configurations. A work triangle consisting of a grill, sink, and work counter suits many outdoor chefs. However, it may be more practical to think in terms of zones: a *hot zone* for grills, wood-burning ovens, and side burners; a *cold zone* for refrigerators, coolers, and ice makers; a *wet zone* for sinks and beverage centers; and a *dry zone* for food preparation and serving. Also consider how these zones relate to each other functionally. At least a little counter space in each zone is helpful, as you always need a place to set down plates, utensils, and your own beverage. When possible, a longer run of counter space is more useful than several short segments.

When laying out the kitchen, it helps to think in terms of modular components, keeping in mind that some are above-counter and others are below-counter. Grills, side burners, and sinks occupy counter space. Storage, refrigeration, warming ovens, and trash receptacles do not. Several under-counter components can be placed side by side to create a stretch of counter space.

top • This unique, V-shaped configuration separates food preparation and service from grilling activities. A wood-burning fireplace is centrally located and serves as a focal point, and a dining table is conveniently located in the open space created by the V.

above • This U-shaped kitchen features a wood-burning oven, gas grill, and ample counter space beneath a raised-bar seating area. The bar can be used for primary seating, overflow seating, or just a place to visit with the chef while dinner is being prepared.

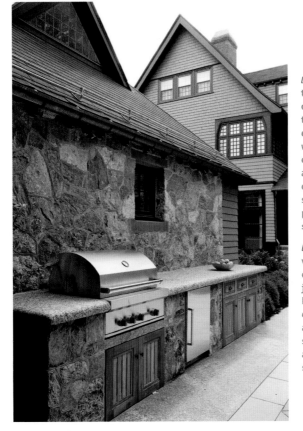

left • Placed against the garage, this outdoor kitchen takes advantage of an existing, eye-catching wall. An under-counter refrigerator and storage cabinets create ample counter space for food preparation and serving.

below • A small, stone-veneered grilling cabinet was located just beyond the kitchen door for convenience. It is also placed away from seating and dining areas to minimize smoke.

Cabinet Layout Options

Single counter

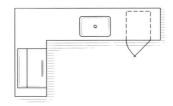

L-shaped counter

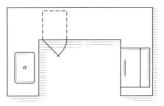

U-shaped counter

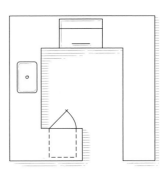

G-shaped counter

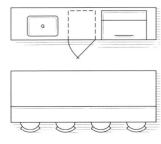

Galley

A Cool Outdoor Kitchen and Dining Patio

Michele Markota loves to cook—indoors and out. Although now that she has an outdoor kitchen with both gas and charcoal grills, she actually prefers cooking and dining al fresco and has postponed a renovation of her indoor kitchen. The gas grill fires up quickly, providing the speed and convenience that is especially welcome on busy weeknights. Even so, she can't imagine cooking a burger over anything except charcoal. Dual grills also double her cooking capacity when needed. Meat can be cooked over the charcoal grill while accompaniments can be prepared on the gas grill.

Of course, it gets hot in Los Angeles—even before firing up two grills—so FormLA landscaping designed a dining arbor adjacent to the outdoor kitchen with retractable shade cloth and a built-in misting system to help keep things cool. A bubbling fountain

along the edge of the patio also makes things seem cooler and more relaxed. The arbor serves another purpose as well—to draw attention away from the rear of the garage, which sits behind the house and adjacent to the patio.

In addition to a round dining table beneath the arbor, the outdoor kitchen features a bump-up bar with seating for four. The bar, which is covered in stone tile, can also be used for serving. The cooking and dining area is built on a patio of concrete pavers edged with a poured-in-place concrete curb. A nearby retaining wall was constructed from concrete recycled from the driveway that was removed during a landscape makeover, while steps and pathways traverse the sloped site, meandering through a low-maintenance garden to several small destination patios.

above • Cooking and dining activities take place on the L-shaped, concrete-paver patio just beyond the garage, while a series of paths lead to smaller, destination seating areas in the landscape. The outdoor kitchen features both gas and charcoal grills along with bar seating.

left • Misters attached to the dining arbor help cool things off on hot summer days. The outdoor kitchen features a stucco-finished cabinet with stone-tile countertops. The raised bar expands seating capacity.

A special feature of the dining arbor is a retractable shade cloth ceiling that helps with temperature control on hot days. From the dining area, guests have a good view of the hillside garden.

Built-in Outdoor Kitchen Cabinets

The odds of finding a one-stop source for cabinetry options are unlikely. Retail stores offer ready-made islands or modular cabinets. Cabinetry makers offer custom wood-frame or modular-framing systems. Landscape designers and contractors are more likely to be familiar with custom masonry framing. Do local research before making a final decision.

READY-MADE GRILLING ISLANDS
$

- Quick and easy installation
- Lighter weight materials
- Limited design options

READY-MADE MODULAR CABINETS
$$

- Mix-and-match design options
- Ample storage available
- Mirrors traditional indoor kitchen styles

MODULAR FRAMING SYSTEMS
$$–$$$

- Flexible design
- Custom finish and counter options
- Ample storage available
- Nonflammable frame

CUSTOM WOOD FRAME CABINETS
$$–$$$

- Most versatile design
- Ample storage available
- Frame is flammable

CUSTOM MASONRY FRAMES
$$–$$$

- More difficult to design
- Extremely durable
- Nonflammable
- Classic outdoor look

These brushed stainless-steel cabinets come as modular units with stainless-steel frames. They can be mixed and matched, and configured as straight runs or with angles to create L- and U-shaped layouts.

A variety of countertops can be placed on most cabinets. These stucco cabinets feature poured, stained concrete countertops, which are set against a low backsplash of decorative glass tiles.

above • Flagstone veneer can be applied to either concrete block or concrete backer board used with modular framing systems. The flagstone on these cabinets matches the adjacent retaining wall. This kitchen also features stone countertops and a farmhouse sink.

left • Block masonry cabinets are easy to build, non-flammable, and can be finished with a variety of veneers. This one features a stacked-stone veneer and stone tile countertop. Storage is generally limited to the open space beneath the grill rather than to drawers and cabinets.

Dining Areas

When designing a dining area, start by identifying the right location—one with adequate space for the number of people you expect to seat. Add 3 ft. to each side of the table for moving chairs or walking behind seated guests to determine the minimum space requirement, adding more for a spacious feeling. The right location should also be convenient to the cooking area and upwind of the grill. And finally, it should be a place with the kind of atmosphere you desire—perhaps open to the stars above, shaded from the setting sun, sheltered from frequent rain showers, enclosed for privacy, or open to distant views.

Tables and chairs are available in a variety of shapes and sizes—bistro tables for 2, round and square tables for 4 or more, and long rectangular tables that seat up to 12. They also come in a wide range of materials and styles, from classic teak designs to more contemporary metal models. Bar seating can also be created at the outdoor kitchen counter, whether it is used for visiting while the chef is grilling, as the primary dining area, or for overflow seating.

Don't forget to consider food service. Grilling islands and bar counters are ideal for this. Waist-height side or buffet tables also work well. If your table is large enough, serving dishes can be placed in the center for passing. Refrigerators, bar sinks, and beverage centers in an outdoor kitchen simplify beverage service. Under-counter trash and recycle bins can help with cleanup.

It's also important to create the right ambience, and one of the best ways to do that is with outdoor lighting—whether candles on the table, downlights hung in trees, a chandelier hanging from an arbor, or accent lighting that highlights adjacent landscape features. In most cases, a combination of lighting types does the trick.

The bright colors, overhead beams, and lush surroundings help make this generously sized dining area feel cozy and inviting. By using benches for seating, this table can easily accommodate different-sized gatherings. Benches can also seat more than chairs, as they occupy less space per person at a table.

above • With a bump-up counter or counter extension, as shown here, an outdoor kitchen can easily double as a dining area. This one easily seats six on stools or in chairs along the side away from the grill.

above • A dining space doesn't have to be large. This one is tucked into a tiny garden patio, yet there is still room to get in and out of the chairs. Even though the space is surrounded by plants, it has a light, airy feeling about it.

left • Furniture options are expanded when dining areas are situated beneath a roof and protected from the weather. This one features a table and chairs you might find indoors. A covered dining area also makes it easier to install lighting and ceiling fans.

Estimating Space Needs

As a general rule, allow more space in an outdoor dining room than you would indoors, as the scale of a patio in relation to the house and surrounding landscape makes it feel smaller than a room in the house. Also, people aren't generally comfortable being positioned close to the edge of a patio, so give them a little breathing room. And finally, keep in mind that for dining room chairs you also need plenty of space to pull them out and step away from the table—an extra 3 ft. on each side of the table is considered a minimum. Here are some common measurements for outdoor dining furniture:

- Bistro table—30 in. to 36 in. dia.
- Round table for 4—48 in. dia.
- Round table for 8—72 in. dia.
- Rectangular table for 6—68 in. long by 36 in. deep
- Rectangular table for 8—72 in. to 90 in. long by 40 in. deep
- Rectangular table for 10—90 in. long by 40 in. deep
- Rectangular table for 12—118 in. long by 40 in. deep
- Arm chair—22 in. to 25 in. wide by 24 in. deep
- Side chair—18 in. wide by 22 in. deep

above · A pull-up counter offers seating for two next to the fireplace, making this a favorite destination for meals any night of the week. The seating arrangement also offers views of the adjacent garden.

right · Food service and cleanup are simplified when dining areas are adjacent to a kitchen or dining room. This one features a painted arbor with a square grid and electrical lighting, which can be easily run from the house.

This sunken patio is tucked in between the house and garden, creating a strong sense of privacy in an in-town neighborhood where lots are narrow and homes are closely spaced. For larger parties, the owners remove the chairs and use the table for serving buffet-style.

ENHANCING

Outdoor spaces are no different from indoor spaces in that family and friends are more likely to gather there if they are warm and inviting.

YOUR OUTDOOR

Outdoor hearths, comfortable furniture, water features, and gardens all help enhance a patio.

SPACE

Outdoor Hearths

Fire is like a magnet—indoors or out, it attracts a crowd. Fire creates the perfect ambience in almost any season. And few things feel better than backing up to a warm fire on a cool evening. While traditional fireplaces offer classic appeal and add a strong architectural element to the landscape, fire pits recreate the ambience of a campfire and allow friends to gather in a circle for easy conversation. And although they don't contribute as much to ambience, portable heaters can be very effective when it comes to warming up a space to extend the evening or season outdoors.

Due to their sheer size and height, fireplaces command attention and serve as focal points on patios. As such, they should be positioned carefully. Once placed, they tend to dictate where everything else goes. And while fireplaces are generally placed along the periphery of the patio, they can often be built against the house. Fire pits, by contrast, have a much lower profile and are placed in more central locations. Due to their size, they are also very suitable to smaller spaces.

Both fireplaces and fire pits can be custom-built on site and finished in stone, brick, tile, or stucco. Both are also available in manufactured versions that can be delivered to your site. Fire pits come in portable units, as well. Patio heaters come in floor, tabletop, and wall-mounted versions, so their placement is flexible.

Wood is the traditional fuel for outdoor fireplaces and generally produces the most heat. It also produces that natural flame, snap, and crackle that is part of the fireplace experience. Yet other fuels are not only available but also more environmentally friendly. Manufactured logs, natural gas, liquid propane, proprietary gels, and bio fuels such as ethanol provide alternatives that produce less smoke, soot, ash, and other airborne particulates, and utilize fewer natural resources.

This custom-built masonry fireplace has a commanding presence in the landscape, clearly serving as the focal point of an outdoor room. The style, materials, and scale are all in keeping with the home.

above · This outdoor hearth is part of the exterior architecture of the house, an important consideration when designing a new home. Unlike most fireplaces, which are centered on a wall, this one is eye-catching because of its off-center placement.

left · Reminiscent of a council ring, this fire pit and surround are constructed from decorative concrete block. The walls help contain the heat, and the built-in seating offers space for many to gather around the fire.

Outdoor Hearths

Although they can help heat up a space, most outdoor hearths are more about adding ambience. They come in a variety of styles and price ranges, and some do a much better job than others when it comes to knocking the chill off an evening.

CUSTOM-BUILT, MASONRY FIREPLACES AND FIRE PITS
$$$
- Stone, brick, tile, and stucco veneers
- Built to your specifications, on site
- Heavy-duty
- Permanent installation

MANUFACTURED FIREPLACES AND FIRE PITS
$$
- Ready-made, freestanding models
- Wide range of styles and finishes
- Lightweight construction, delivered to site

PATIO HEATERS
$$
- Portable
- Floor, tabletop, and wall-mount models
- Lack the ambience of a flickering fire
- Most efficient heat production

PORTABLE FIRE DISHES
$
- Fire dish, chiminea, fire pit, luminaria
- Great for small spaces
- Portable

above • This stone hearth has a unique curved opening, and the wide raised hearth offers plenty of seating up close to the fire. A raised hearth helps place the heat where you need it most—at body level rather than at ground level.

Portable, wood-burning fire pits are affordable, readily available, and convenient, as they can be moved easily about a patio depending on outdoor activities. This one has a decorative tile finish on a wrought-iron base.

above • This contemporary, custom-designed table features a flame fueled by liquid ethanol and surrounded by tempered glass. Liquid ethanol burns cleanly and efficiently; it does not produce ash, smoke, or soot and cleans up easily.

left • The flame and heat intensity of this gas fire pit can be adjusted easily with a turnkey control. It's easy to light and can be quickly turned off when it's time to call it a night, since there's no waiting around for the coals to die down.

Masonry Fireplaces

Stone is, by far, the most popular choice for masonry fireplaces. However, fireplaces can also be veneered with brick, tile, or stucco. They can require a substantial investment, but they also make a strong architectural statement in the landscape and can provide many hours of outdoor enjoyment, as people always love to gather around a hearth.

1. The mantel and chimney of this riverstone fireplace offer a place to display several of the homeowners' favorite pieces of artwork. The fireplace was added when the raised patio and overhead roof were constructed. 2. Ventless fireplace alternatives such as natural gas, liquid propane, proprietary gels, and bio fuels provide unique design opportunities that don't require chimneys. This one features cut-granite slabs for the hearth, mantle, and fireplace surrounds. 3. Mantles are just as welcome on outdoor fireplaces as on indoor fireplaces. Whether built-in or attached, they add dimension, provide a decorative accent, and create a shelf for displaying artwork or other items. 4. This stone fireplace looks and feels as if it belongs in the Tuscan countryside. It provides warmth and atmosphere for casual outdoor gatherings around a large dinner table, where the furnishings have been carefully chosen to complement the stone.

Fire Pits

The primary difference between fire pits and fireplaces is that you can gather in a circle around fire pits like you would a campfire. But fire pits, like fireplaces, can be set at or above ground level, designed to suit any style, made from a wide range of materials, and fueled by wood, gas, gels, or bio fuels.

1. This sleek, contemporary design provides an unexpected architectural element to the pool deck. The bed of small river cobbles covers the gas burners, creating an almost mysterious source for the flames. 2. Campfires don't have to be built in the ground or in the center of an open area. They also can be created in freestanding or built-in dishes, such as this one, along the periphery of a patio. The rustic metal back on this one reflects heat and helps call attention to the flame. 3. This gas fire pit was built into the stone seat wall along one side of a pool deck. Although the logs look real, their flame is easily adjusted from a small control panel. This end of the pool deck also features a dining area, outdoor kitchen, and covered bar. 4. Burners on gas fire pits come in rings, rods, stars, and other configurations that produce multiple flames. As the burner on this contemporary fire pit shows, such configurations can produce very natural-looking flame.

Gathering around the Hearth

Evenings can get cool, even in sunny southern California. Yet evening is a favorite time for these homeowners to spend time outdoors—relaxing with family, watching the sun set over the canyon, or enjoying Fourth of July fireworks. Their teenaged children enjoy inviting friends over to hang out, and the patio is their favorite spot to gather. The fire pit helps make that possible, or at least more comfortable, by knocking off the gentle chill and adding ambience to any evening.

Designed by Katie Moss and Jorge Salazar of Katie Moss Landscape Design, the rectangular patio is paved in cement tiles that were poured especially for the home, which is a mid-century modern that was designed by an architect for himself. The cement tiles have been used both indoors and out to create a sense of continuity. (Cement tiles are a form of concrete that use a very fine aggregate such as marble powder. The result is a tile with the strength of concrete and a very smooth finish.)

The fire pit and L-shaped seat wall, which blend in nicely with the paving, were constructed with recycled concrete. In fact, 80 percent of the materials used throughout the entire landscape for paths, steps, retaining walls, and even an outdoor kitchen, were recycled. The fire pit has an H-shaped burner that warms the lava rocks that help hold in the heat. It is fueled by natural gas. The patio seats eight comfortably in chairs and another four to six on the seat wall.

top • This fire pit and nearby seat wall were both constructed from recycled concrete, while the patio flooring features poured concrete pavers that match flooring inside the home. The fire burns natural gas, and the burner rod is covered with small, dark river cobbles.

right • A seat wall anchors one corner of the patio, providing extra seating and defining the outer boundary. Like the fire pit, it was constructed from recycled concrete that has a smooth surface and rough, textured sides.

Not too big, yet not too small, this patio is just the right size—in scale with the house and with ample room for a small party. There is seating for nearly a dozen and standing room around the fire for many more.

Outdoor Lighting

For a truly welcoming front entry or inviting outdoor room, landscape lighting can help create an atmosphere that is subtle rather than bold or glaring, casting the right kind of light where you need it most. Landscape lighting falls into two broad categories—functional and atmospheric. Functional lighting makes it safe to move about and allows you to see what you're doing. It includes general, task, path, and step lighting. Atmospheric lighting creates ambience, establishes a mood, and accents architectural or garden features. It includes both accent and ambient lighting.

For safety, adequate lighting on paths and steps is essential. Soft, evenly spaced lights that cast their beam down and out are most effective. The beams should overlap slightly to create an evenly lit surface. Path and step lights are important at transitional areas. For short flights of steps, lights placed at both the top and bottom of the steps may be sufficient. For longer flights, built-in wall or tread lights may also be needed.

Soft downlights placed overhead provide adequate lighting on parking areas and many paths.

Patios benefit from a broader range of lighting types. Downlights placed in trees, against the house, or on overhead structures provide general lighting. Task lights are helpful where cooking, serving, or other activities take place. Ambient lighting—whether candles, tea lights strung in trees, or a softly illuminated chandelier—will create a romantic atmosphere for dining. And accent lighting can add drama by uplighting trees or casting attention on water features, garden sculpture, or architectural details.

It is less disruptive to add landscape lighting when constructing paths and patios because the work involves digging holes and trenches. Yet even in a mature landscape, adding proper lighting can make a difference in how much you enjoy your patio after dark.

above · Integrated step lights are an unobtrusive and effective way to illuminate grade changes after dark. They can be installed in either the step or an adjacent wall, but must be planned for in advance and installed during construction.

above · A pair of wall-mounted, wrought-iron sconces with frosted shades provides a soft glow over this grill and side burner. There is just enough light for the task at hand without making the grill the focal point of the landscape.

left · Both path lights and wall lights illuminate the way on this patio. The house lights also play a key role, providing soft ambient light. The flames from this raised, rectangular fire pit also brighten this outdoor space.

right · The warm glow of candlelight and fire light warms up a cool evening on the waterfront. Positioning a patio, such as this council ring, near a body of water also capitalizes on the sunset and moonlight reflecting off the water.

Outdoor Lighting

Outdoor lighting generally falls into five basic functional categories. Throughout the landscape and even just on a patio, each of these different types will likely be needed. It's not so much one type instead of another, but several types in combination with each other that creates a safe and inviting outdoor environment.

GENERAL LIGHTING
$–$$$
- Broad beam coverage
- Soft, overall illumination for outdoor spaces
- Place high in a tree, on an eave, or against a wall

TASK LIGHTING
$–$$$
- Narrow beam coverage
- Bright, functional illumination
- Casts light on a specific activity such as grilling
- Place near and slightly above work area

PATH AND STEP LIGHTING
$–$$
- Broad beam coverage
- Soft light on paths and steps
- Mount on small posts or low walls

ACCENT LIGHTING
$–$$
- Narrow beam coverage, often from two directions
- Bright light that calls attention to illuminated object
- Highlights trees, fountains, sculptures, and other features
- Fixtures often placed on ground

AMBIENT LIGHTING
$
- Low, soft, and sometimes flickering lights
- Used to create mood
- Candles, torches, string lights

above • This wall-mounted task light complements the styling of the cabinetry, countertops, and sink, providing just the right amount of light for preparing food or rinsing dishes in the large basin sink.

above • Uplights placed on the ground and aimed at the tree canopy turn small, ornamental trees into sculptural objects in the night landscape. Two small lights per tree do the trick.

above • Path lights are placed along this walkway that spans a small reflecting pool and waterfall. However, ambient light spilling from the house is often the primary source of light. It also provides bright reflections on the pool.

left • Mission-style lanterns and wall lamps help carry out the Arts-and-Crafts theme echoed in the fence and arbor design while softly illuminating the pool deck and dining area. The translucent shades provide a soft, warm glow.

Furnishings

No patio is complete until it is furnished. Top billing goes to outdoor furniture, because to relax and enjoy a space, you need a place to sit. Furniture is also a way to show your sense of style and to help set the mood for an outdoor room—whether you prefer the classic look of teak, the rustic simplicity of twigs, or the more contemporary flair of galvanized aluminum. In addition to style, consider durability. Outdoor furniture takes a beating, so choose materials that won't rust, rot, stain, splinter, peel, or fade. Pieces should be heavy enough that they won't blow over in a storm, but light enough to be rearranged or stored under cover for winter.

Consider the types of furniture you need: Sofas, chairs, dining sets, chaise longues, benches, bar stools, hammocks, swings, rockers, and gliders are all possibilities for seating. Several good tables will also come in handy for eating, setting down drinks and books, displaying favorite objects, or playing games. Consider special seating, dining, or play areas designated specifically for children, too.

Beyond furniture, consider other items that can dress up a space and make it more inviting. Water features can help mask unwanted sounds and create a soothing atmosphere. Statuary, sundials, and sculpture can serve as focal points and conversation starters. Gardens—whether in-ground borders, planting pockets, raised beds, or container gardens—can soften paved surfaces. Gardens that are all green and white create an especially relaxed and calming atmosphere, while colorful flowers can bring a space to life. Fragrant flowers are especially welcome in courtyard and patio settings. Decorative items can also add interest—a vase of fresh flowers, outdoor rugs, pillows, found objects, unique lighting fixtures, or even mirrors (which can make a small space look larger).

Outdoor furnishings can be just as comfortable as those designed for indoor use. The deep cushions on these chaise longues almost demand an afternoon nap, and the nearby bubbling fountain helps set just the right tone.

above • Hand-wrought chairs and a tile tabletop help establish a casual, free-spirited atmosphere in this southwestern courtyard garden. The colors in the tile and seat cushions are echoed in the surrounding plant foliage and flowers, while the lantern makes a subtle accent.

top left • These sleek, contemporary, hardwood chairs have mesh seats and backs, and the table features a wood top and metal legs. The combination of wood stain, mesh, and metal all work to pull together the outdoor furniture, architecture, and grill for a unified look.

bottom left • All-weather wicker comes in a range of styles and colors. These brightly colored chairs and ottoman are complemented by cushions and pillows crafted from equally weather-resistant fabrics.

Weather-Worthy Outdoor Furniture

Outdoor furniture should be built to withstand the elements—water and humidity, prolonged sun exposure, hard freezes, and extreme temperature swings. Cushions and fabrics, too, should be chosen for their resistance to mildew, rot, and fading. Choose from furniture materials that suit both your style and climate demands.

ALUMINUM
$

- Lightweight tubular aluminum and heavier solid aluminum
- Rust resistant; will whiten and pit
- Can get hot or cold, depending on weather
- Hard surface; cushions add comfort

IRON
$$

- Heavy to move around yet heavy-duty, sturdy
- Paint or powder-coat to prevent rusting
- Can get hot or cold, depending on weather
- Hard surface; cushions add comfort

PLASTIC
$–$$

- Resin or recycled-plastic construction
- Lightweight, often stackable
- Easy to clean
- Available in many any colors

WOOD
$$–$$$

- Rot-resistant teak and tropical hardwoods most durable
- Cedar, redwood, cypress, and pressure-treated pine most affordable
- Quality crafted pieces are sturdy and durable
- Can be heavy and bulky
- Lifespan varies depending on wood and quality of construction
- Paint, stain, or leave natural finish

WOVEN
$$

- Marine-varnished reeds, plastic-wrapped fiber, acrylic strips
- Sturdy metal frame with woven exterior finish
- Medium weight
- Lasts up to 30 years
- Comfortable with or without cushions

right • The bright blue and white furnishings echo the colors in the sky and call to mind a marine setting. The oversized market umbrella provides a spot of shade and some protection from a sudden, light rain shower.

facing page left • Galvanized-steel sheet metal covers this table, providing a smooth, rust-resistant surface. The metal chairs can be painted or allowed to rust for a weathered look, though the rust should be sanded to prevent staining or tearing clothing.

bottom • Wooden furniture made from cedar, redwood, or teak—such as these long-backed Adirondacks—never goes out of style in the garden. The chairs have a classic, simple look and comfort that remains appealing.

below • The design of wrought-iron furniture has changed significantly over the years. These powder-coated chairs are contemporary in design and softened with plush, weather-resistant cushions.

ORNAMENTS AND ART

Sculpture, sundials, statuary, unique found objects, and interesting architectural fragments can help give an outdoor space personality. They can be placed as focal points, conversation pieces, or surprise elements on a patio or along a garden path. They could also be placed farther into the landscape—perhaps on the lawn or in a perennial border—as part of a framed view from the patio. An architectural element might be hung on a garden or house wall, while a striking sculpture rises up out of a flower bed. Smaller objects might sit on tables or be tucked into a container planting. Multiple items could be clustered together to create a vignette or spaced strategically along a walkway to draw you deeper into the garden.

Regardless of what you add, try to keep it simple—especially when objects are also competing with the landscape itself. Seek out objects that have meaning to you and reflect your sense of style.

above • Simple, earth-toned objects such as metal lanterns, glass bottles, and velvety pillows combine to give this adobe architecture textural accents without overpowering the beauty of its clean lines and styling.

right • A large wall sculpture is the focal point of this small brick patio. Despite its size, the sculpture blends in rather than standing out too boldly because its dark color recedes in the landscape.

above • These lamps and other objects could just have easily been used indoors. Because they are covered by the large overhang of the portico roof, they will be mostly protected from the weather. Wiring should be rated for outdoor use.

WATER FEATURES

Bubbling stones, gently spouting fountains, and cascading water walls are a luring element in any landscape. Tucked into a patio, they help soothe nerves at the end of a stressful day at work and mask the sounds of cars, ringing phones, or power equipment so often heard in today's neighborhoods. Fish ponds add a mesmerizing element to a patio and are favorites among children. With or without fish, a small fountain or pool can attract birds, butterflies, and frogs where they can be observed and enjoyed. A wide range of plants that love wet feet can also be added to larger basins or pools of water. But even a simple basin of still water reflecting clouds moving across the sky can add a delightful element to an outdoor room.

Anything that holds water can serve as a basin. For sound, bubbling stones and containers require the least amount of water and are among the easiest water features to install and maintain. Garden centers sell many units that simply need to be filled with water and plugged into a nearby outlet, or you can easily make your own with a container, pump, and a little creativity. Landscape designers and contractors can help design and build more architectural features—raised brick reflecting pools, sheet waterfalls, or narrow runnels that channel water across the patio floor. Designs can be classic, contemporary, or naturalistic to match the surrounding space, home, or landscape.

Water features are wonderful elements to include at a home's front entry. What better way is there to greet guests than by giving them something interesting to look at and soothing to listen to while they wait at your front door! Water features can also be placed alongside paths, as focal points at the end of garden paths, or as the centerpiece of a formal courtyard.

facing page top • Wall fountains like this one come fully assembled, ready to be hung on a wall as a focal point. An outlet is located nearby to provide electricity for the recirculating pump.

facing page bottom • This powder-coated cauldron was fitted with a fountain and perched over a small pool. The water simply recycles, providing a continuous, soothing sound near the patio.

above • Large pots and urns are easily turned into bubbling fountains. The catch basin for the water is located beneath these pots, hidden by the river cobbles. Having the pair of pots helps lead one through the landscape.

GARDENS AND CONTAINERS

In addition to being destinations, patios are also transitional spaces between a house and the surrounding landscape. They are used as if they were another room of the home, yet they are outdoors—surrounded by sky, trees, and lawns. Perhaps the best way to visually connect a patio to the surrounding landscape is with plants. This can be done by edging the patio with garden beds, integrating planting pockets into the patio's surface, building raised beds in the patio that bring plants closer to eye level, or planting in containers.

Planting beds are easy to design. Just leave a 2-ft. or deeper border between the paved patio and a boundary wall. If there are no walls, dig planting beds 3 ft. to 4 ft. wide just beyond the patio's boundaries. Small planting pockets can be created in corners, along the edge of a swimming pool, or randomly in any patio by leaving small spaces (sometimes just a foot or more in width) without paving. In older, dry-laid patios, pavers can often be removed to create planting pockets. Drought-tolerant plants such as succulents, small ornamental grasses, and herbs are ideal for these petite spaces. New or existing patios can be fitted with raised beds made from brick, stone, or other masonry materials, then filled with soil and plants. The slope beyond a retaining wall can be planted, as well.

Planted containers are suitable on any patio, as well as along pathways and flanking doorways, and the containers themselves can be chosen to tie in with the colors or style of the architecture. Other than requiring frequent watering, containers are easy to tend. They can be updated seasonally or planted with perennials, shrubs, and small trees that will last for many years.

above · Dozens of pots filled with perennials have been clustered on this patio to create an above-ground garden. By packing the pots densely and emphasizing foliage plants for long-season good looks, one can achieve a look as lush as an in-ground garden.

left · In addition to surrounding the pool deck with an extensive garden, planting pockets have been added closer to the pool's edge to break up the expanses of stone paving and to help create a more naturalistic setting.

right · Containers can be every bit as beautiful as the plants placed in them. This one is both decorative and colorful, as cobalt blue is among the most striking colors to place in the landscape. It grabs attention in much the same way red or white do in a garden.

A Southwest Courtyard Garden

Just a stone's throw from historic Canyon Road in Santa Fe, New Mexico, Catherine Clemens and Bill Peterson live in a rambling old adobe home that backs up to the Acequia Madre, or "mother ditch," a stone-lined irrigation canal built by Spanish settlers in the 1600s. Both the home and surrounding property are divided into a multitude of spaces that have been used for various purposes over the years. As a landscape designer, Catherine is tackling the outdoor spaces one at a time. Her first target since moving into this home was the entry courtyard, accessed from the parking court through an aged wooden gate with ample southwestern character.

This pass-through space doubles as an outdoor living area. Surrounded by adobe walls and with worn bricks underfoot, it feels warm and cozy and offers a strong sense of privacy. Tall cottonwood trees provide an overhead canopy. Yet with a generous opening along one wall into the side lawn, the patio still feels open and spacious. The round table is a regular dining spot for family and friends, and the two lounge chairs provide a place to relax with a good book. A bubbling urn beckons guests and the homeowners alike into the courtyard.

Although the desert Southwest is a mostly dry landscape, courtyard gardens are common. This one features a winding raised bed made from stacked stone, as well as dozens of generously planted clay containers. There are spots of brightly colored flowers, especially in summertime, but the emphasis here is on the foliage, which provides long-season good looks. Vines scramble up and over the walls, while old lanterns and other antiques are tucked here and there for accent.

above • Clusters of containers and a raised, stacked-stone planting bed hug the walls of this entry courtyard, creating an inviting view from both the main entry and kitchen. The opening on the far right wall leads to an adjacent garden space with a lawn.

right • Containers filled with reliable foliage plants such as coleus, geraniums, and begonias offer color and interest in the garden long after their brightly colored flowers have faded. The clay containers blend in with the bricks and adobe walls.

above • A bubbling urn serves as a focal point in the raised bed. Its sound attracts birds, as well as guests and the homeowners, to this lush garden spot in the Southwest desert. Bubbling containers and stones use only a minimum of water, which is recycled in an underground basin.

left • Two broad, shallow steps and a pair of terra-cotta urns mark the transition from the lawn to the courtyard garden. The path leads past the dining table to the front door (right) and kitchen (left), which has double doors that open wide onto the patio.

Containers

Inexpensive pots can provide a good home for plants just as well as their pricier cousins, so use your container budget wisely, keeping in mind that quality has more to do with looks and longevity than adaptability. Choose decorative containers for key locations while hiding others in the background or with trailing plants.

CERAMIC
$–$$

- Broadest range of shapes, styles, and finishes
- Breakable if dropped
- Can crack with freeze-thaw cycles

CLAY
$–$$

- High-fired terra-cotta containers most durable
- Low-fired terra-cotta containers crack and flake with freeze-thaw cycles
- Breakable
- Porous—allows plant roots to breath
- Classic and decorative styles

CONCRETE
$–$$

- Nearly indestructible
- Heavy, difficult to move
- Can chip

METAL
$$–$$$

- Iron, aluminum, galvanized steel, stainless steel, copper
- Can be classic or contemporary in design
- Best in shady locations, as metal heats up and can burn plant roots

PLASTIC
$

- Inexpensive
- May be molded into various styles and colors
- Lightweight
- Not breathable

STONE
$$$

- Durable
- Classic good looks
- Heavy

SYNTHETIC
$–$$

- Foam, resin, molded plastic
- Mimics more expensive pots in looks
- Durable, yet lightweight
- Waterproof, rot-proof, impact-resistant
- Wide range of styles and finishes

WOOD
$$–$$$

- Classic and rustic styles available
- Redwood, cedar, and teak are most common woods
- Must maintain to prolong life
- Paint, stain, and/or seal

above · They are heavy and can be difficult to move, but concrete planters rank among the most durable pots. These two have been molded with decorative patterns, planted with boxwood and ivy, and placed next to a front door.

right · Although it has the styling of a classic wooden box planter, this container is actually made of fiberglass for strength and durability. It is finished in an automotive-grade paint that is resistant to UV rays and scratching. Drip irrigation keeps the soil moist without wasting water.

facing page top right · High-fired terra-cotta pots from Italy come in decorative designs and are more durable than their more common terra-cotta cousins. These rolled-rim pots are filled with a variety of small shrubs, ornamental grasses, and tropical foliage plants.

facing page bottom right · A single, striking container planting can make a strong statement in the landscape. This tall ceramic planter is filled with a trailing fanflower, a heat- and drought-tolerant annual that blooms all season long. It greets visitors in a front entry courtyard.

RESOURCES

Design

CLEMENS & ASSOCIATES, INC.
Landscape design
www.clemensandassociates.com

DA VIDA POOLS, LLC
Pool and spa design
www.davidapools.com

DAVID THORNE LANDSCAPE ARCHITECTS
Landscape architecture
www.thornela.com

THE FOCKELE GARDEN COMPANY
Landscape and garden design
www.fockelegardencompany.com

FORMLA
Landscape design
www.formlainc.com

GROUPWORKS, LLC
Pools and spa design
www.groupworksllc.com

HABERSHAM GARDENS
Landscape design
www.habershamgardens.com

JENI WEBBER LANDSCAPE ARCHITECT
Landscape architecture and sustainable garden design
www.jeniwebber.com

KATIE MOSS LANDSCAPE DESIGN
Landscape design
www.katiemoss.com

OUTER SPACES
Landscape architecture and pool design
www.outerspacesinc.com

RED ROCK CONTRACTORS, LLC
Pool and spa design
www.buildredrock.com

RICHARD MCPHERSON LANDSCAPE ARCHITECTURE
Landscape architecture
www.rmcpherson.com

Outdoor Kitchens

BARBECUES GALORE
www.bbqgalore.com

EARTHSTONE WOOD-FIRE OVENS
www.earthstoneovens.com

FOGAZZO
www.fogazzo.com

FORNO BRAVO
www.fornobravo.com

GRILL KITCHENS
www.grillkitchens.com

HEARTHSIDE FIREPLACE, PATIO AND BARBECUE CENTER
www.hearthsidedistributors.com

MUGNAINI IMPORTS
www.mugnaini.com

OUTDOOR KITCHEN DISTRIBUTORS, INC.
www.outdoorkitchen.com

THE OUTDOOR KITCHEN STORE
www.outdoorkitchenstore.com

SUPERIOR CLAY CORPORATION
www.superiorclay.com

TEXAS PIT CRAFTERS
www.texaspitcrafters.com

Outdoor Hearths

BUCKLEY RUMFORD COMPANY
www.rumford.com

CALIFORNIA OUTDOOR CONCEPTS
www.californiaoutdoorconcepts.com

FIRE PIT SHOP
www.firepits.com

NEXO
www.nexofireplace.com

VERMONT CASTINGS
www.myownbbq.com

Outdoor Lighting and Sound

BOSE
www.bose.com

CRUTCHFIELD
www.crutchfield.com

GRAND LIGHT LIGHTING AND DESIGN
www.grandlight.com

KICHLER LIGHTING
www.kichler.com

LIGHTHOUSE LANDSCAPE LIGHTING
www.lightsbylighthouse.com

THE OUTDOOR LIGHTS
www.theoutdoorlights.com

OUTDOOR LIGHTING
www.outdoorlighting.com

OUTDOOR LIGHTING PERSPECTIVES
www.outdoorlights.com

SEA GULL LIGHTING
www.seagulllighting.com

Arbors and Shade Structures

ABSOLUTE AWNINGS
www.absoluteawnings.com

AWNINGS.US
www.awnings.us

DALTON PAVILIONS, INC.
www.daltonpavilions.com

GAZEBO CREATIONS
www.gazebocreations.com

SAFARI
www.safarithatch.com

SHADE SAILS
www.shadesails.com

SUMMERWOOD PRODUCTS
www.summerwood.com

TAYLORMADE AWNING
www.taylormadeawning.com

VIXEN HILL CEDAR PRODUCTS
www.vixenhill.com

CREDITS

p. ii (left to right): © Brian Vanden Brink; design: Dominic Mercadante, Architect; © Mark Lohman; © Brian Vanden Brink, design: Horiuchi & Solien, Landscape Architects; © Lee Anne White, design: Clemens & Associates; © Mark Lohman

p. iii (left to right): © Brian Vanden Brink, design: Will Winkelman, Architect/Roger Christopher Design, LLC; © Lee Anne White; © Eric Roth; © Jennifer Cheung Photography, design: Gabriela Yariv Landscape Designer, www.gabrielayariv.com; © Jennifer Cheung Photography

p. 2: top (left to right): © Eric Roth; © Brian Vanden Brink, design: Siemasko + Verbridge; © Lee Anne White, design: David Feix; © Chris Giles, design: Katie Fragan, Katie Moss Design; © Lee Anne White; bottom: © Mark Lohman

p. 3: © Lee Anne White

CHAPTER 1

p. 4: © Eric Roth

p. 6-7: © Brian Vanden Brink, design: Polhemus Savery DaSilva Architects Builders

p. 7: top: © Jennifer Cheung Photography, design: Sandy Koepke, www.sandykoepkeinteriordesign.com; bottom: © Lee Anne White, design: Clemens & Associates, homeowner: George Goldstein

p. 8: top: © Brian Vanden Brink, design: Dominic Mercadante, Architect; bottom: © Jennifer Cheung Photography, design: Gabriela Yariv Landscape Designer, www.gabrielayariv.com

p. 9: top: © Jennifer Cheung Photography; bottom: © Lee Anne White, design: Clemens & Associates, homeowners: Steve and Deena Koundouriotis

p. 10: © Lee Anne White, design: Hillary Curtis and David Thorne, David Thorne Landscape Architect

p. 11: © Brian Vanden Brink, design: The Green Company

p. 12: top: © Brian Vanden Brink, design: Ennead Architects; bottom: © Jennifer Cheung Photography, design: Gabriela Yariv Landscape Designer, www.gabrielayariv.com

p. 13: top: © Lee Anne White, design: Jeni Webber, homeowners: Tom and Diane McBroom; bottom: © Mark Lohman

p. 14: top: © Chris Giles, design: Jeni Webber, Landscape Architect; bottom: © Chris Giles, design: Jeni Webber, Landscape Architect

p. 15: © Chris Giles, design: Jeni Webber, Landscape Architect

p. 16: © Eric Roth

p. 17: © Lee Anne White

CHAPTER 2

p. 18: © Mark Lohman, design: Janet Lohman Interior Design

p. 20: © Lee Anne White, homeowners: Tim and Claudia Birningham

p. 21: left: © Lee Anne White; right: © Brian Vanden Brink, design: Group 3, Architects/Hankin Group, Builder

p. 22: © Brian Vanden Brink, design: Polhemus Savery DaSilva Architects Builders

p. 23: © Eric Roth; design: www.miskovskylandscaping.com

p. 24: left: © Brian Vanden Brink, design: Sally Weston, Architect; right: © Jennifer Cheung Photography, design: Gabriela Yariv Landscape Designer, www.gabrielayariv.com

p. 25: © Eric Roth

p. 26: © Chris Giles, design: Cassy Aoyagi, FormLA

p. 27: left: © Chris Giles, design: Cassy Aoyagi, FormLA; right: © Chris Giles, design: Cassy Aoyagi, FormLA

p. 28: © Jennifer Cheung Photography, design: Elizabeth Przygoda, Landscape Design, www.boxhilldesign.com

p. 29: bottom: © Mark Lohman; top: © Eric Roth, design: www.christinetuttle.com

p. 30: top: © Mark Lohman, design: Harte Brownlee & Associates; bottom left: © Brian Vanden Brink, design: Horiuchi & Solien, Landscape Architects; bottom right: © Jennifer Cheung Photography, design: Sandy Koepke, www.sandykoepkeinteriordesign.com

p. 32: © Lee Anne White, design: Red Rock Contractors

p. 33: top: © Mark Lohman, design: Chateau Sonoma; bottom: © Eric Roth, design: www.LDARCHITECTS.com

p. 34: © Eric Roth, design: www.whitlabrothers.com

p. 35: © Lee Anne White, homeowners: Mary and Dana Streep

p. 36: top: © Eric Roth, design: www.columbiacon.com; bottom: © Eric Roth, design: www.spacecraftarch.com

p. 37: © Eric Roth, design: www.jkennard.com

p. 39: top: © Eric Roth; bottom: © Eric Roth, design: www.robinkramergardendesign.com

p. 40: top: © Eric Roth; center: © Mick Hales; bottom: © Lee Anne White, design: Bill Caldwell, Harrison Design Associates, Habersham Gardens

p. 41: © Brian Vanden Brink, design: Hutker Architects, Horiuchi & Solien Landscape Architects

p. 42: © Mick Hales

p. 43: top: © Lee Anne White, design: Kristina Kessel and David Thorne, David Thorne Landscape Architect; bottom: © Lee Anne White, homeowners: Carl and Kim Spadaro

p. 44: © Susan Teare, design: George Zavis, HGC Landscape and Architectural Design, hg-c.com

p. 45: top: © Lee Anne White, design: Da Vida Pools; bottom: © Mark Lohman, design: Bravado Design

p. 47: top: © Jennifer Cheung and Steven Nilsson Photography, design: Rick Button, ASL; bottom left: © Jennifer Cheung Photography; bottom right: © Eric Roth

p. 48: left: © Mark Lohman; right: © Eric Roth, design: www.LombardiDesign.com

p. 49: right: © Brian Vanden Brink

p. 50: top: © Lee Anne White. design: Harrison Design Associates, M. E. Nochols Construction; bottom: © Lee Anne White, design: Pools by John Clarkson, homeowners: Carl and Kim Spadaro

p. 51: © Lee Anne White, design: David Feix

p. 52 © Jennifer Cheung Photography, design: Brian Kissinger, Landscape design, www.thomasandtodd.com

p. 53: top: © Lee Anne White, design: Red Rock Contractors; bottom: © Jennifer Cheung Photography, design: Gabriela Yariv Landscape Designer, www.gabrielayariv.com

p. 54: © Mark Lohman

p. 55: © Jennifer Cheung Photography, design: Brooke Deitrich, Landscape design, www.greenlandscapestoenvy.com

p. 56: left: © Lee Anne White; right: © Brian Vanden Brink, design: Horiuchi & Solien Landscape Architects

p. 57: top: © Jennifer Cheung and Steven Nilsson Photography, design: Heather Lenkin Landscape Designer, www.lenkindesign.com; bottom: © Eric Roth, design: www.horstbuchanan.com

CHAPTER 3

p. 58: © Jennifer Cheung Photography, design: Sandy Koepke, www.sandykoepkeinteriordesign.com

p. 60: top: © Brian Vanden Brink, design: Whitten Architects; bottom: © Mark Lohman, design: Barclay Butera Inc.

p. 61: top: © Eric Roth; bottom: © Lee Anne White, design: Red Rock Contractors

p. 62: top © Brian Vanden Brink, design; Hutker Architects, bottom Jennifer Cheung Photography

p. 63: top: © Mark Lohman; bottom: © Susan Teare, design: George Zavis, HGC Landscape and Architectural Design, hg-c.com

p. 64: top: Lee Anne White, design: Clemens & Associates; bottom: Lee Anne White, design: Clemens & Associates

p. 65: © Lee Anne White

p. 66: © Jennifer Cheung and Steven Nilsson Photography, design: Heather Lenkin Landscape Designer, www.lenkindesign.com

p. 67: top left: Lee Anne White, design: Red Rock Contractors; top right: Mark Lohman; bottom: Jennifer Cheung Photography, design: Gabriela Yariv Landscape Designer, www.gabrielayariv.com

p. 68: © Lee Anne White, design: Fired Up Kitchens; bottom: © Mark Lohman

p. 69: © Brian Vanden Brink

p. 70: © Brian Vanden Brink, design: Will Winkelman, Architect/Roger Christopher Design, LLC

p. 71: top: © Jennifer Cheung Photography, design: Sandy Koepke, www.sandykoepkeinteriordesign.com; bottom: © Eric Roth, design: www.kl-la.com

p. 72: © Eric Roth, design: www.deckhouse.com

p. 73: top: © Mick Hales; bottom: © Lee Anne White, design: Red Rock Contractors

p. 74: top: © Brian Vanden Brink, design: Scholz & Barclay Architects; bottom: © Eric Roth

p. 75: © Jennifer Cheung Photography

p. 76: © Mark Lohman

p. 77: top: © Lee Anne White, design: Groupworks; bottom: © Brian Vanden Brink

p. 78: top: © Lee Anne White, design: The Fockele Garden Company, homeowners: Alexander and Janet Patterson; bottom: © Lee Anne White, design: The Fockele Garden Company, homeowners: Alexander and Janet Patterson

p. 79: © Lee Anne White, design: The Fockele Garden Company, homeowners: Alexander and Janet Patterson

p. 80: © Eric Roth, design: www.bhbrowndesign.com

p. 81: top: © Lee Anne White, design: Clemens & Associates; bottom: © Eric Roth

p. 82: top: © Lee Anne White, design: Jeni Webber; bottom left: © Chris Giles, Katie Fragan, Katie Moss Design; bottom right: © Jennifer Cheung and Steven Nilsson Photography, Rick Button, ASLA

p. 83: © Lee Anne White, design: The Fockele Garden Company, homeowners: Dan and Benny Moss

p. 84: top: © Lee Anne White, design: Hillary Curtis and David Thorne, David Thorne Landscape Architect; bottom: © Jennifer Cheung Photography, design: Brian Kissinger, Landscape design, www.thomasandtodd.com

p. 85: top: © Lee Anne White, design: Da Vida Pools; bottom: © Lee Anne White

p. 86: top left: © Lee Anne White, design: DaVida Pools, homeowners: Ritchy and Julie Scoggin; top right: © Lee Anne White, design: DaVida Pools, homeowners: Ritchy and Julie Scoggin; bottom: © Lee Anne White, design: DaVida Pools, homeowners: Ritchy and Julie Scoggin

p. 87: right: © Lee Anne White, design: DaVida Pools, homeowners: Ritchy and Julie Scoggin

p. 88 top: © Eric Roth, design: www.sternmccafferty.com; bottom: © Lee Anne White, design: Erdreich Architecture

p. 89: © Mark Lohman

p. 90: top: © Brian Vanden Brink, design: Hutker Architects, Horiuchi & Solien Landscape Architects; bottom: © Susan Teare, design: George Zavis, HGC Landscape and Architectural Design, hg-c.com

p. 91: top: © Susan Teare, landscape design and installation: Rich and Rachel Boyers; bottom: © Mark Lohman

CHAPTER 4

p. 92: © Mark Lohman

p. 94: top: © Lee Anne White, design: Frances Dixon; bottom: © Mark Lohman

p. 95: left: © Brian Vanden Brink, design: The McDowell Company; right: © Lee Anne White, homeowner: Sally Faulkner

p. 96: left: © Jennifer Cheung Photography, desisgn: Gabriela Yariv Landscape Designer, www.gabrielayariv.com; right: © Susan Teare, design and installation: Church Hill Landscapes, Inc.

p. 97: © Mark Lohman

p. 98: © Lee Anne White

p. 99: top: © Lee Anne White, design: Clemens & Associates, homeowners: Scott and Rita Karns; bottom: © Lee Anne White, design: Harrison Design Associates, M. E. Nichols Construction, Habersham Gardens

p. 100: © Jennifer Cheung Photography

p. 101: top: © Lee Anne White, design: Paula Refi, build: The Fockele Garden Company; bottom left: © Brian Vanden Brink, design: Hutker Architects, Horiuchi & Solien Landscape Architects; bottom right: © Jennifer Cheung Photography, design: Jason Isenberg Landscape Design,www.realmenvironments.com

p. 103: top left: © Lee Anne White, design: Clemens & Associates, homeowners: Roy and Tana Bidwell; top right: © Lee Anne White, design: Clemens & Associates, homeowners: Roy and Tana Bidwell; bottom: © Lee Anne White, design: Clemens & Associates, homeowners: Roy and Tana Bidwell

p. 104: © Jennifer Cheung and Steven Nilsson Photography, design: Heather Lenkin Landscape Designer, www.lenkindesign.com

p. 105: left: © Lee Anne White, design: The Fockele Garden Company, homeowners: Alexander

and Janet Patterson; right: © Jennifer Cheung Photography, design: Elizabeth Przygoda, Landscape Design, www.boxhilldesign.com

p. 106: top: © Lee Anne White, design: Clemens & Associates, homeowners: Steve & Deena Koundouriotis; bottom: © Jennifer Cheung Photography, design: Gabriela Yariv Landscape Designer, www.gabrielayariv.com

p. 107: top: © Mark Lohman; bottom: © Jennifer Cheung and Steven Nilsson Photography, design: Rick Button, ASLA

p. 108: © Lee Anne White, design: Pools by John Clarkson

p. 109: left: © Mark Lohman; top right: © Lee Anne White; bottom right: © Lee Anne White

p. 110: top: © Eric Roth; bottom: © Lee Anne White, design: Da Vida Pools, homeowners: Jon and Marci Aune

p. 111: left: © Mark Lohman; right: © Mark Lohman

p. 112: top: © Lee Anne White, design: Got-U-Covered Interior Design, homeowners: Joy and Ned LeBlanc; bottom: © Lee Anne White, design: Got-U-Covered Interior Design, homeowners: Joy and Ned LeBlanc

p. 113: © Lee Anne White, design: Got-U-Covered Interior Design, homeowners: Joy and Ned LeBlanc

p. 114: top: © Lee Anne White, design: Harrison Design Associates, M. E. Nichols Construction, Habersham Gardens; bottom: © Mick Hales

p. 115: © Lee Anne White, design: Red Rock Contractors

CHAPTER 5

p. 116: © Lee Anne White, design: Bill Caldwell, Harrison Design Associates, M. E. Nichols Construction, Habersham Gardens

p. 118: left: © Jennifer Cheung Photography, design: Gabriela Yariv Landscape Designer, www.gabrielayariv.com; right: © Susan Teare, design: J. Graham Goldsmith Architects

p. 119: © Brian Vanden Brink, design: H.P. Rovinelli Architects

p. 120: top: © Eric Roth, design: hutkerarchitects.com; bottom: © Susan Teare, design and installation: Church Hill Landscapes, Inc.

p. 121: right: © Mark Lohman

p. 122: left: © Lee Anne White, design: Bill Caldwell, Harrison Design Associates, M. E. Nichols Construction, Habersham Gardens; right: © Eric Roth, design: www.svdesign.com

p. 123: © Susan Teare, design: Cushman Design Group and Asa Searles from Eden Vermont

p. 124: top: © Mark Lohman; bottom: © Brian Vanden Brink, design: Horiuchi & Solien, Landscape Architects

p. 125: top: © Lee Anne White, design: Hillary Curtis and David Thorne, David Thorne Landscape Architect; bottom: © Jennifer Cheung Photography, design: Brian Kissinger, Landscape Design

p. 126: top: © Chris Giles, design: Richard McPherson, Landscape Architect; bottom: © Chris Giles, design: Richard McPherson, Landscape Architect

p. 127: © Chris Giles, design: Richard McPherson, Landscape Architect

p. 128 top: © Mick Hales; bottom: © Lee Anne White, design: Hillary Curtis and David Thorne, David Thorne Landscape Architect

p. 129: © Lee Anne White, homeowner: Randi Herman

p. 130: © Jennifer Cheung and Steven Nilsson Photography, design: Heather Lenkin Landscape Designer, www.lenkindesign.com

p. 131: top: © Lee Anne White, design: Graham Pittman & Associates, Habersham Gardens; bottom left: © Mark Lohman; bottom right: © Lee Anne White

p. 132: © Lee Anne White, homeowner: Randi Herman

p. 133: top left: © Mark Lohman; top right: © Brian Vanden Brink, design: Weatherend Estate Furniture;bottom: © Mark Lohman

p. 134: top: © Lee Anne White, design: Four Dimensions Landscape; bottom: © Lee Anne White, design: Jeni Webber

p. 135: © Lee Anne White, design: Anne Sheldon

p. 136: © Eric Roth, design: www.jwconstructioninc.com

p. 137: top left: © Brian Vanden Brink, design: Horiuchi & Solien, Landscape Architects/John Colomarino, Architect; top right: © Lee Anne White, design: Clemens & Associates, homeowner: George Goldstein; bottom: © Lee Anne White, design: Bill Caldwell, Harrison Design Associates, Habersham Gardens

p. 138: top: © Mark Lohman; bottom: © Lee Anne White, design: Bill Caldwell, Harrison Design Associates, Habersham Gardens

p. 139: top: © Brian Vanden Brink, design: Horiuchi & Solien, Landscape Architects; bottom © Mick Hales

p. 140: © Jennifer Cheung Photography

p. 141: top: © Jennifer Cheung Photography, design: Gabriela Yariv Landscape Designer, www.gabrielayariv.com; bottom: © Mick Hales

p. 142: © Jennifer Cheung Photography

p. 143: top: © Lee Anne White, design: Groupworks; bottom: © Mick Hales

p. 144: left: © Brian Vanden Brink, design: Howell Custom Building Group; right: © Mark Lohman

p. 145: top: © Lee Anne White, design: Clemens & Associates, homeowner: George Goldstein; bottom: © Mark Lohman

p. 146: left: © Lee Anne White, design: Betty Ajay; right: © Mark Lohman

p. 147: left: © Lee Anne White, design: Bill Caldwell, Harrison Design Associates, Habersham Gardens; right: © Brian Vanden Brink, design: Will Winkelman, Architect

p. 148: left: © Lee Anne White; top right: © Jennifer Cheung Photography, design: Gabriela Yariv Landscape Designer, www.gabrielayariv.com; bottom right: © Brian Vanden Brink, design: Phi Home Designs

p. 149: © Lee Anne White, design: Jeni Webber

p. 150: top: © Brian Vanden Brink, design: Coastal Designers & Consultants Inc., builder: Knickerbocker; bottom: © Mark Lohman

p. 151: top: © Susan Teare, design: Cushman Design Group and Bruce Paine of P&P Landscaping from Morrisville Vermont; bottom: © Lee Anne White, design: P.O.P.S. Landscaping

CHAPTER 6

p. 152: © Lee Anne White, design: Clemens & Associates, homeowners: Scott and Rita Karns

p. 154: © Lee Anne White

p. 155: top left: © Jennifer Cheung Photography, design: Sandy Koepke, www.sandykoepkeinteriordesign.com; top right: © Lee Anne White, design: Da Vida Pools, homeowners: Jon and Marci Aune; bottom: © Lee Anne White, design: Clemens & Associates, homeowner: George Goldstein

p. 156: top: © Chris Giles, design: Katie Fragan, Katie Moss Design; bottom: © Lee Anne White, design: Da Vida Pools

p. 157: top: © Mark Lohman, bottom right: © Brian Vanden Brink, design: Horiuchi & Solien, Landscape Architects

p. 158: top: © Chris Giles, design: Katie Fragan, Katie Moss Design; bottom: © Jennifer Cheung Photography

p. 159: top: © Eric Roth, design: www.shconstruction.com; bottom: © Lee Anne White, homeowners: Gary and Carolyn Palmer

p. 160: © Chris Giles, design: Cassy Aoyagi FormLA, homeowner: Michele Ann Markota

p. 161: top: © Chris Giles, design: Cassy Aoyagi, FormLA, homeowner: Michele Ann Markota; bottom: © Chris Giles, design: Cassy Aoyagi, FormLA, homeowner: Michele Ann Markota

p. 162: © Jennifer Cheung Photography, design: Sandy Koepke, www.sandykoepkeinteriordesign.com

p. 163: top left: © Chris Giles, design: Cassy Aoyagi, FormLA; bottom left: © Lee Anne White, design: Red Rock Contractors; right: © Jennifer Cheung Photography, design: Gabriela Yariv Landscape Designer, www.gabrielayariv.com

p. 164: © Mark Lohman

p. 165: top: © Lee Anne White, design: Da Vida Pools; bottom left: © Lee Anne White, homeowners: Carol and Kim Spadaro; bottom right: © Mark Lohman, design: Rob Proctor

p. 166: left: © Mark Lohman; right: © Mark Lohman

p. 167: © Lee Anne White, design: Anne Sheldon

CHAPTER 7

p. 168: © Mark Lohman

p. 170: © Jennifer Cheung Photography, design: Gabriela Yariv Landscape Designer, www.gabrielayariv.com

p. 171: top: © Eric Roth; bottom: © Jennifer Cheung and Steven Nilsson Photography, design: Heather Lenkin Landscape Designer, www.lenkindesign.com

p. 172: top: © Lee Anne White, design: Red Rock Contractors; bottom: © Lee Anne White

p. 173: left: © Lee Anne White, design: Red Rock Contractors; right: © Lee Anne White, design: Clemens & Associates, homeowners: Steve and Deena Koundouriotis

p. 174: top: © Lee Anne White, design: Clemens & Associates, homeowner: George Goldstein; bottom: © Eric Roth, design: www.shconstruction.com

p. 175: left: © Mark Lohman; right: © Jennifer Cheung Photography, design: Gabriela Yariv Landscape Designer, www.gabrielayariv.com

p. 176: left: © Jennifer Cheung Photography, design: Glen Brouwer, Integration Design Studio; right: © Jennifer Cheung Photography, design: Elizabeth Przygoda, Landscape Design, www.boxhilldesign.com

p. 177: top: © Lee Anne White, design: Hillary Curtis and David Thorne, David Thorne Landscape Architect; bottom: © Susan Teare, design: H. Keith Wagner Partnership Landscape Architects and Blazing Designs, Inc.

p. 178: top: © Chris Giles, design: Katie Fragan, Katie Moss Design; bottom: © Chris Giles, design: Katie Fragan, Katie Moss Design

p. 179: © Chris Giles, design: Katie Fragan, Katie Moss Design

p. 180: © Eric Roth, design: www.christinetuttle.com

p. 181: top left: © Lee Anne White, design: Red Rock Contractors; top right: © Lee Anne White, design: Red Rock Contractors; bottom: © Brian Vanden Brink, design: Siemasko + Verbridge

p. 182: top: © Jennifer Cheung Photography, design: Sandy Koepke, www.sandykoepkeinteriordesign.com; bottom: © Eric Roth, design: www.LDARCHITECTS.com

p. 183: top: © Brian Vanden Brink, design: Group 3, builder: Hankin Group; bottom: © Jennifer Cheung Photography, design: Gabriela Yariv Landscape Designer, www.gabrielayariv.com

p. 184: © Lee Anne White, design: Red Rock Contractors

p. 185: top left: © Jennifer Cheung Photography; bottom left: © Eric Roth; right: © Jennifer Cheung Photography, design: Elizabeth Przygoda, Landscape Design, www.boxhilldesign.com

p. 186: © Eric Roth

p. 187: left: © Jennifer Cheung Photography, design: Sandy Koepke, www.sandykoepkeinteriordesign.com; top right: © Lee Anne White; bottom right: © Susan Teare, landscape design and installation: Rich and Rachel Boyers

p. 188: left: © Lee Anne White, homeowners: Mary and Dana Streep; right: © Jennifer Cheung Photography, design: Elizabeth Przygoda, Landscape Design, www.boxhilldesign.com

p. 189: © Jennifer Cheung Photography

p. 190: top: © Mark Lohman; bottom: © Lee Anne White

p. 191: © Mark Lohman

p. 192-193: © Mark Lohman, design: Rob Proctor

p. 192: bottom: © Mark Lohman, design: Rob Proctor

p. 193: right: © Mark Lohman, design: Janet Lohman Interior Design

p. 194-195: © Lee Anne White, design: Catherine Clemens, homeowners: Catherine Clemens and Bill Peterson

p. 194: bottom: © Lee Anne White, design: Catherine Clemens, homeowners: Catherine Clemens and Bill Peterson

p. 195: top: © Lee Anne White, design: Catherine Clemens, homeowners: Catherine Clemens and Bill Peterson; bottom: © Lee Anne White, design: Catherine Clemens, homeowners: Catherine Clemens and Bill Peterson

p. 196: © Jennifer Cheung Photography, design: Gabriela Yariv Landscape Designer, www.gabrielayariv.com

p. 197: left: © Lee Anne White, design: Kristina Kessel, David Thorne Landscape Architect; top right: © Lee Anne White, design: Catherine Clemens; bottom right: © Lee Anne White, design: Clemens & Associates, homeowners: Scott and Rita Karns

INDEX